Other PC World Books

Getting Started with the IBM PC and XT
by David Arnold and the Editors of PC World

How to Buy an IBM PC or Compatible Computer

Danny Goodman
and the Editors of PC World

PC World Books
Published by
Computer Book Division
Simon & Schuster, Inc.
New York

Copyright © 1984 by Danny Goodman
and PC World Communications, Inc.

Published by the Computer Book Division
Simon & Schuster, Inc.
Simon & Schuster Building
Rockefeller Center
1230 Avenue of the Americas
New York, New York 10020

SIMON AND SCHUSTER and colophon are registered
trademarks of Simon & Schuster, Inc.
PC World and colophon are trademarks of
PC World Communications, Inc.

Manufactured in the United States of America

10 9 8 7 6 5 4 3 2 1

Library of Congress Cataloging in Publication Data

Goodman, Danny
  How to buy an IBM PC or compatible computer.

  Includes index.
    1. IBM Personal Computer. 2. IBM Personal Computer XT
3. Microcomputers—Purchasing. I. PC world. II. Title.
III. Title: How to buy an I.B.M. P.C. or compatible computer.
QA76.8.I2594G67   1984   001.64   84-1383

ISBN   0-671-49282-9

To Al Levy

Contents

Preface

We all go through it at some time during our lives. When we need to make a major purchase, such as an automobile, a house, or an air conditioner, we talk to friends, study consumer magazines, and consult salespeople. But after it's too late, we realize that we didn't know enough to ask the right questions. The car, we find out, is nearly impossible to service routinely without special tools. We didn't think to ask for a geologist's report on the fissure-ridden land under the house. And the air conditioner—purchased on sale—requires special wiring in the house before it can be used.

Buying an IBM Personal Computer or one of the dozens of compatibles is similarly laden with pitfalls. Preparing for the kinds of decisions that you will face as you assemble a system requires considerably more than reading a few magazine reviews.

When I bought my IBM PC in 1981, one month after the machine was first available, my choices were limited, since just about anything I could plug into the computer was available only from IBM. No matter how inefficient a particular plug-in board or piece of software was, it was the only choice at the time. Nevertheless, I chose the PC from the few professional computers available then, betting that the IBM microcomputer would be a popular system that would attract many software and hardware developers.

To my surprise and delight, the industry responded with more products and choices during the first year than I expected after two. I wish, however, that I had known all the choices I was to have; I would certainly have configured my system differently.

Now that so many options are available, I think it's important to have one convenient volume that covers everything a potential PC buyer should know. In this book I present all the questions you should ask both yourself and the salespeople in computer stores. Three months from now you won't be muttering "I wish I'd known that," as many PC owners have done.

Since I made my own purchasing decisions in buying an IBM PC, dozens of friends and acquaintances have asked for advice and guidance in outfitting their PC or PC-compatible computers. I have listened carefully to those who have experienced both the joys and the sorrows of owning a PC in all its possible configurations. The answers provided in this book are to the questions and the problems I have encountered over the years. Among those whom I remember with fondness are Lawrence J. Magid, Jeremy Joan Hewes, John Miron, J. David Wertman, Gerald Barinholtz, Ricardo Barrett, and the staff at the Sears Business Systems Center in Arlington Heights, Illinois. We all learned together. Special thanks go to Steven Cook and Robert Luhn for their independent studies of PC compatibility. And the biggest thanks go to Linda, whose patience and understanding are unequaled.

How to Buy an IBM PC or Compatible Computer

The PC in Perspective

Since you are reading this book, you obviously have an interest in personal computing. You have probably decided that an IBM Personal Computer or PC-compatible computer is the way to go. You may not know much about the inner workings of computers, or you may be an experienced user about to graduate from a less powerful system or from a home computer. Whatever your particular case, welcome to this exploration of the complex and often confusing choices offered by IBM PC-standard computers. ("PC-standard computers" is used throughout this book to refer to the IBM PC and PC-compatible computers.)

Pre-IBM

When you consider that personal computers have been around since the mid-1970s and that the first products were targeted at technically experienced hobbyists, you can't help but marvel at the rapid pace with which personal computers have been accepted as work tools for business people and students. The Apple II computer, which first appeared in its familiar shape in 1977, established a solid foundation for today's popularity of computers in schools, homes, and laboratories. Business people soon began to recognize Apple's breakthrough in making useful, small computers affordable at the consumer level, particularly when *VisiCalc* (VisiCorp), the pioneering spreadsheet program, was introduced. Other manufacturers began to produce software tools, such as *AppleWriter* (Apple) and *pfs:file* and *pfs: report* (Software Publishing), that offered scaled-down versions of mainframe and minicomputer programs.

But it was largely self-employed professionals, small-business owners, and maverick executives who brought computers into the office. One significant group of business people declined to participate in this original personal computer revolution: the large corporations.

Enter IBM

In August 1981, IBM announced the IBM Personal Computer. Technologically, it was not a radically new kind of computer. One of IBM's primary claims, that the PC uses a 16-bit microprocessor chip, even bent the rules a bit. Although the IBM PC employed a 16-bit microprocessor—a technological advance over the 8-bit microprocessor used in almost all personal computers up to that time—the PC does not take full advantage of that chip's capabilities.

To understand this point, let's consider some fundamentals of computer operation. Computer circuits communicate with one another by sending streams of "on" and "off" signals (very low voltage electrical pulses) literally millions of times per second. It's like sending signals to a friend in the dark by switching a flashlight on and off according to a predetermined code. Programmers have assigned the numbers 1 and 0 to these on-off voltage states. In contrast to the 1 to 10 decimal numbering system (consisting of the numbers 0 through 9), only two numbers, 1 and 0, make up the binary numbering system. Each number (corresponding to an "on" or an "off" pulse) represents a binary digit, abbreviated *bit*. The smallest unit of information racing through the chips inside a computer is represented as a 1 or a 0—a bit.

Eight-bit microprocessors move information through the computer in groups of eight bits, along eight parallel lines. Technological purists, then, would assume that a 16-bit computer moves 16 data bits simultaneously. In the IBM PC, however, that is only partially true.

Inside the PC's microprocessor, called the 8088 by its manufacturer, Intel Corporation, information is handled in 16-bit groups. But outside the chip (connections to the keyboard, the disk drives, the monitor, and so on), information travels in 8-bit groups. In fact, according to an Intel executive, IBM—not Intel—called the 8088 a 16-bit chip.

The advantage of a true 16-bit computer—data moving in groups of 16 bits throughout—is usually increased speed in processing and transferring information from one part of the computer to another (other factors also affect speed). But because the PC is partially an 8-bit computer running at a conservative pace regulated by its internal clock (the built-in timer that determines how quickly bits move through the system), it is not a front-runner in the speed derby.

One benefit of having the 16-bit internal structure, however, is that the PC can use much more memory at any moment than an 8-bit computer. (Chapter 2 will explore memory in greater detail.) An 8-bit computer is generally limited to using 64 kilobytes (1 kilobyte equals 1024 characters) of memory. Because the PC can handle up to 1 megabyte (1000K) of memory without doing any fancy tricks, it has room for larger, more sophisticated applications programs than 8-bit computers have. For applications that require complex calculations, long documents, or complicated color graphics, having additional memory on tap is essential.

Increased memory capacity alone is not usually enough to sustain a new personal computer in the marketplace. But aside from this feature, the IBM PC offered little more than previous business personal computers. It came into the world with only a handful of software packages, and it could not run software used with the other computers on the market. Nor did its pricing break any barriers; a typical business system cost at least $3000. So why was the PC an overnight success?

The Name of the Game

The PC's success did not lie in its technology—it was in the IBM name on the cabinet. To most consumers, the IBM name conjures up pictures of room-sized computers. But to corporate purchasers, many of whom already owned or leased IBM equipment, the IBM name suggested tangible benefits of high-quality engineering and superior after-sale support. It followed, then, that whatever IBM did in personal computers would fall in line with the company's reputation for producing reliable products. Buying IBM was safe—especially if you already had IBM equipment in-house.

Early confidence in the PC from within the corporate community led major software developers to produce an avalanche of productivity-oriented software. The first programs available for the PC were largely translations of software that ran on 8-bit computers. These programs served as important stopgaps by providing useful software for a computer that suddenly became popular among executives, small-business owners, and professionals. The rapid appearance of software contributed to the PC's popularity, which in turn encouraged further software development, and the PC phenomenon snowballed.

Not all the early action was in software, however. The PC's design shared one element that was also at the root of the Apple II's success: hardware expansion slots. Expansion slots inside a computer enable owners to add circuit boards to meet the demands of specific applications. In the PC, expansion slots play a critical role in getting the computer to operate in a useful configuration.

A number of hardware designers saw an opportunity to produce expansion products for the PC, augmenting IBM's limited and expensive selection of plug-in cards. Some hardware suppliers began combining several functions onto single boards (called multifunction boards), and other suppliers offered memory upgrades at prices considerably lower than IBM's. Increased hardware support threw yet more fuel into the corporate and professional fires burning for the PC.

Within a year after IBM announced the PC, the machine was commanding a share of the market that surprised even IBM. Demand frequently outstripped supply, no matter how much IBM increased production. At about the same time, a new phenomenon surfaced: the PC-compatible computer.

Round Two

At a November 1982 trade show in Las Vegas, the computer industry had an opportunity to see working prototypes of several computers ready to ride on the coattails of IBM. Manufacturers of the machines claimed software or hardware compatibility with the PC based on hardware specifications. These computers distinguished themselves from the PC in portability, price, and features. As you will see in Chapter 12, compatibility claims for such computers should be scrutinized carefully.

But the blossoming of the compatible computers and the vast amount of software and hardware for the PC demonstrate that the IBM PC has evolved into a kind of standard. Even if a computer manufacturer does not claim PC compatibility, the machine will probably be measured against the PC. Today, practically every new personal computer intended for professional use employs the 8088 microprocessor, its true 16-bit cousin, the Intel 8086, or the newest additions to the family, the 80186 and the 80188. Many machines' cabinet designs bear a striking resemblance to the PC's, and virtually all of them run software configured for MS-DOS, a generic version of the disk operating system originally developed for the PC (see Chapter 9 for a discussion of disk operating systems).

As the PC evolves, other compatibles are sure to follow. Few companies are likely to have such an unprecedented, pervasive effect on the personal computer marketplace. Although IBM may find a new direction for future PC models, the company is not likely to forsake the entrepreneurs who helped make the PC the informal standard it is. That fact should comfort those who might hesitate to buy a computer today for fear that it may become obsolete tomorrow. A PC-standard computer represents a solid, long-term investment in personal computing.

It's Your Turn

This industry-wide commitment to PC-standard computers offers so many choices that you may have trouble sifting through the combination of advertising hype and your own inclinations. One of the first decisions this book will help you make is whether you need a PC, the Portable PC, or the more substantially powered XT. Having made that decision, you will then choose between a computer bearing the IBM logo or a machine claiming PC compatibility.

Regardless of the outcome of these first two decisions, the third—and most difficult—will involve selecting products that make the computer system a productive tool for your applications. Your initial computer purchase is very critical, because the components you choose (perhaps before you have enough expertise to make informed selections) will affect how your computer will pay for itself in the long run. After all, you don't want to have to discard or sell at a loss products that prove inadequate for later needs. You will have problems only if you are unaware of the long-term impact of these early decisions.

Piece by Piece

With rare exceptions, you will have to assemble a PC system from several composite parts. The personal computer you buy— especially if it is an IBM—will probably be a core machine to which you add a monitor, disk drives, memory, and other items. You will have many options, which may be important later, after you have become familiar with your system and want to extend its capabilities.

This book will help you build your PC system from the ground up or choose a fully configured PC-compatible computer. Chapter 1 introduces the IBM PC and XT and compatible computers. Chapters 2 through 8 examine the hardware options available to you as a potential PC buyer. Chapter 2 discusses how to determine the amount of memory you will need for your applications. Chapters 3 and 4 examine floppy and hard disk drives, and Chapter 5 will clear up any confusion you have about the various display devices used by computers. Chapters 6 and 7 focus on printers and modems, and how to select what you need. Chapter 8 examines the expandability of PC-standard computers and offers advice on conserving their precious expansion slots.

Chapter 9 introduces you to the world of disk operating systems, so that as soon as you start using your computer, you will be able to master DOS. Chapter 10 will help you decide which programming language to learn if programming interests you.

Chapter 11 offers an overview of the PC configuration you will need, depending on the applications you plan for your computer. It also provides guidelines for preserving your system's flexibility, so that it will be able to grow along with your changing needs.

PC compatibility is the subject of Chapter 12. This chapter describes the different degrees of compatibility and provides a synopsis of more than a dozen PC compatibles and how they measure up to the IBM models. This chapter will also help you decide whether to buy the PC or a compatible.

Chapter 13 presents the criteria for choosing a computer dealer. As you will see, this is no trivial matter. Nor is the subject of maintenance contracts; you will learn about their costs, and whether they are worth the additional expense.

Chapters 14 and 15 answer questions you didn't know you should ask. You will learn about the kinds of supplies you'll need right away, and how to design the most efficient environment for your computer.

Some of the advice in this book does not represent the most economical alternative in the short term. It is wise to consider long-term savings, in both money and peace of mind. The more you use your computer, the more you will rely on it. Saving $100 on a system by choosing a substitute component is no savings at all if that component breaks down in the middle of an important job.

The goal of this book is to help you put together a reliable system that will provide years of service and allow you to expand it sensibly as your awareness of its power grows and your needs change. If you understand your options before you buy, your electronic partner will expand with you—not hold you back. Planning is the key to PC happiness.

PCs, XTs, and Compatibles

Buying an IBM Personal Computer or a compatible involves more than you may expect—more than buying a television, for example. With a TV, your choices are limited by the amount of space you can devote to it and the amount you can spend on it. Once you make the choice, you bring the TV home, take it out of the box, plug it in, and it does everything it was designed to do without further effort on your part.

What makes buying a PC-standard computer more difficult than buying most other equipment is that the process forces you to make a number of decisions for which, by and large, you are unprepared. And the decisions you make while shopping will affect your future with the computer. Some of the decisions are as fundamental as whether to buy an IBM machine or a computer that is reputedly compatible with the IBM. Other decisions, such as how much memory to add, may seem esoteric now, but in one or two years they may actually have a more profound effect on your work than the brand of computer selected. This chapter presents a summary of the major choices you will have to confront. The chapters that follow take a closer look at the components and choices required in assembling a computer system.

Figure 1.1 *The IBM PC, along with two compatibles: the Eagle PC desktop computer and the Texas Instruments portable machine.*

The IBM PCs

The IBM PC comes in two basic styles: desktop (including the PC and XT models) and portable. The desktop PC consists of a main console (called the System Unit), which contains one or two floppy disk drives and a separate typewriter-style keyboard connected to the System Unit by a cable. The desktop PC does not come with a monitor, however. You can choose either the IBM Monochrome Display or Color Display (or another manufacturer's monitor) and add the appropriate plug-in adapter board to the PC to complete the system. The basic PC System Unit contains 64K of RAM, but you can purchase more memory with the computer if you want. The System Unit contains five expansion slots into which plug-in boards can be inserted, but two of these slots are occupied by adapter boards for the disk drive(s) and the monitor.

The IBM XT is an enhanced version of the desktop PC. It consists of a System Unit, the keyboard, at least 128K of RAM, one built-in floppy disk drive, and a built-in hard disk. As with the PC, you must choose either the Monochrome Display or the Color Display separately and add the appropriate plug-in adapter board for the monitor. The XT contains eight usable expansion slots, although the slots are slightly narrower than those of the PC, and two are too short for standard-length plug-in boards. One additional feature of the XT is that it comes with a communications adapter, a short plug-in board that fits into one of the XT's short expansion slots. Three of the XT's long slots are occupied by adapter boards for the floppy disk drive, the hard disk, and the monitor.

The Portable PC is configured somewhat differently. It has one or two floppy disk drives, 256K of RAM, and a built-in 9-inch monochrome monitor that displays both text and graphics in amber (in contrast to the green of the Monochrome Display available for the desktop PC). The Portable also contains the IBM Color/Graphics Adapter, which is needed for the built-in monitor. The Portable PC has eight expansion slots, although one is currently not usable and two others are devoted to the adapters for the monitor and the disk drive(s). Expandability of the Portable is somewhat complicated, however, because four of the five active expansion slots not already filled in the computer are short and cannot accommodate the standard-length plug-in boards most commonly used with the PC.

The Compatibles

Many PC-compatible computers mimic the IBM models—the PC, the XT, and the Portable PC—in general appearance and features. The manufacturers of still other computers claim some degree of compatibility with the IBM models, although they do not duplicate those machines' features and operations as closely. In fact, compatibility between the IBM Personal Computers and the machines offered by other manufacturers varies widely. Regardless of their degree of compatibility, however, many of these machines are sold at lower prices and have more built-in features than the IBM computers. This book refers to the PC-compatible computers collectively as *PC-standard computers.*

Although Chapter 12 discusses compatibility in detail and introduces a number of PC-standard computers, a brief summary here should help establish the essential ways in which non-IBM computers can be compatible with the PC. First, and the most desirable if you want the closest thing to complete compatibility, are the machines that run the majority of programs made for the PC without modification. Among this rather limited group of computers, there is some variation as to the amount of PC software that operates properly on them. A second, larger group of machines uses the same disk operating system as the PC and can therefore run many of the same programs, but to work on the compatibles those programs usually must be modified by the software manufacturer, and you will have to buy the version tailored to your specific machine.

A third group of machines has disk operating system compatibility and some software compatibility with the PC, but they differ in hardware. Two computers in this group use disks that are smaller than the PC's (3½ inches in diameter rather than 5¼ inches), and some other machines use the same disks as the PC but store information differently on the disks.

Another important consideration in choosing a PC-standard system is expandability. The IBM PC has five slots for expansion boards, and the Portable and the XT each have eight expansion slots. Some compatible machines contain expansion slots like those of the IBM machines, but others have little or no room for expansion. You should know the kind of work you will be doing with the computer and the enhancements you will need for that work before you decide on a particular machine.

Portable Configurations

Ever since Adam Osborne called his suitcase-sized Osborne 1 computer "portable," many manufacturers, including IBM, have designed similar computers. But calling a 20- to 32-pound computer portable seems inappropriate when you consider that several computers on the market are small enough to fit inside a briefcase. A better word for these larger portables is *transportable,* since their propensity to be self-contained allows them to be moved to a new location more easily than a desktop computer. Although the transportables are too heavy and bulky to carry for extended periods or tote along comfortably on an airplane, they pack up easily for transporting in a vehicle for limited business travel, and they are designed to handle the shocks involved in moving.

Nearly every portable PC-standard computer comes with a built-in monitor and at least one floppy disk drive. The IBM Portable PC comes with an amber screen, and it can display graphics. The Compaq has a green screen that can reproduce both the high-resolution monochrome text displayed on the IBM Monochrome Display and high-resolution graphics (in green only), depending on the kind of software you use. The computer also has built-in connectors for attaching color monitors. To someone who uses an IBM PC or XT in the office with the text-only Monochrome Display, the Compaq's ability to replicate the same quality and green tint might be more desirable than having to adapt to the IBM Portable's less distinct amber display. Because the portables include a number of features, be sure to choose a model with the ones that are right for you.

If the portable is going to be your primary computer (not a second one for home use or for travel), you might prefer one that offers the most expansion slots, so that you can configure it much like you would a comparable desktop computer. Be sure to find out exactly what kind of expansion boards you can add. The cramped quarters of some portables limit you to adding only one or two full-length expansion boards—the most predominant variety when it comes to practical multifunction boards (those that place several functions on one board to conserve slots).

Some people buy portables because their work station is limited or because they like the way a particular portable looks. Personal reasons for choosing one computer over another are just as valid as technical reasons, as long as you will feel comfortable with the final choice.

Assembling the System

Choosing among the various brands of computers—IBM and the compatibles—and assembling a computer system require a series of decisions. The first decision you will have to make is about the type of work for which you will use the computer. Then you can match the components to your needs.

The second decision you will face is whether to add to the memory already installed on the computer's main circuit board, and how much memory to add. Then, you must plan for the kind of disk drive storage you need (both now and in the future). Will two floppy disk drives be enough? Should they be single- or double-sided? Perhaps your applications will need the vastly increased storage of a hard disk. If so, you can install a hard disk inside the PC System Unit, add an external hard disk to the PC, or consider an XT, which comes equipped with an internal hard disk.

Monitor choices are among the most confusing, primarily because PC-standard computers offer more ways to display text and graphics than most other computers. Each kind of monitor generally requires a different plug-in board inside the System Unit to convert computer signals for display on that particular kind of monitor.

Text is most readable when it is displayed on a monitor that is designed for it, such as the IBM Monochrome Display (which requires the plug-in Monochrome Display Adapter board). If your work is entirely text oriented, you may want to choose between green and amber screens (green or amber characters, respectively, against a black background).

Displaying graphic images, such as pie charts and those used in games, requires a different kind of display adapter inside the System Unit. The need for graphics increases the number of choices you will have to make in selecting a monitor. Not recommended, but entirely possible, is displaying the output from your PC on a color TV (for which you will also need an adapter called an RF modulator). Higher quality images are achieved with a special color display called a composite video monitor. The best color, however, comes from the most expensive type of color display, called an RGB display. (The pros and cons of each are discussed in Chapter 5.)

The final graphics display possibility is using a less expensive monochrome graphics monitor (not the same as the special text-only IBM Monochrome Display mentioned above). Although this type of monitor doesn't display color, it displays graphics at a relatively low cost. What further complicates matters is that a few popular software products work with one kind of graphics monitor but not with others.

Although you can use a color monitor to display text, the color device cannot reproduce text as crisply as a monochrome monitor can. Many users who need both text and color graphics install two monitors at their work stations. If color is not essential in your graphics applications, a monochrome monitor that can display graphics is often a good compromise, even though the text displayed on it isn't as sharp as that of the IBM Monochrome Display.

IBM or Not IBM?

There's little question that the entire group of PC-standard computers is affected by the steps IBM takes. In their desire to be compatible with IBM, other manufacturers have followed "Big Blue" in supplying increased disk storage capacity and more capable disk operating systems. But no matter how hard they try, designers of PC compatibles will never be able to be 100 percent compatible with the original without infringing on IBM's copyrights.

Perhaps the most practical argument for considering a compatible is that many models are less expensive for fully configured systems. Such models are often preconfigured at the factory, reducing, if not eliminating, much of the agonizing decision making that goes into assembling an IBM system. Another incentive for a PC compatible might be that the manufacturer includes (bundles) a selection of software with the computer. Not only has the manufacturer made a number of hardware decisions, but it has also saved the customer hours of software shopping for some useful applications programs. The disadvantage is that the software included with a computer might not be the best for your specific needs. A computer salesperson who helps you assemble a system might direct you to programs more fitting to your line of work. But at least with a bundled system you know exactly what a fully configured system with software costs.

The manufacturers of PC compatibles try to build in attractive features that differentiate their computers from the IBM models, while maintaining a modicum of PC compatibility. Some machines use higher capacity floppy disk drives so that more information can be stored on a single disk. Others use a more advanced version of the PC's 8088 microprocessor chip (the Intel 80186 is a popular substitute) to improve the speed of computations.

The further a computer's design strays from the IBM original, however, the less compatible it is likely to be with the PC. Although such diversity is certainly no sin, if you expect to experiment with software, you may not find the program you want in a format that lets you run it successfully on your machine. You will also be dependent on that one computer manufacturer to keep converting software programs to operate on that computer. And if the company doesn't have the wherewithal to survive the hotly competitive PC marketplace, you may end up with a computer that has no prospects for new software development. Corporate obsolescence can be as tricky as technological obsolescence.

Buying a PC-standard computer should not be taken lightly. It takes a thorough understanding of the necessary choices and how your decisions will affect your use of the computer over the next few years. Although the decisions may involve some guesswork at times, the more prepared you are to deal with your evolving working relationship with the computer, the better you'll be able to handle the changes that come along.

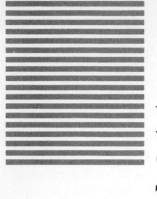

Essential Computer Terms

Bit   An abbreviated form of the words *binary digit,* the most elementary form of data in the computer. Eight bits make up 1 byte.

Board   Any printed circuit board that can be installed in one of the PC or XT expansion slots. (The term *card* is also used to describe such a component.)

Byte   One character of data used by the computer—a letter, a number, or a symbol. Each byte consists of 8 bits.

Command   An instruction to the computer used in conjunction with a program, a language, or the disk operating system.

Cursor   The location indicator on the computer screen. On the PC and the XT the cursor is usually a blinking underscore symbol one character wide (depending on the program being used).

Disk   The principal data storage medium used by the PC and the XT. The floppy disk (called a diskette in the IBM manuals) used in standard systems is a removable mylar disk in a cardboard jacket that measures 5¼ inches in diameter. The XT also has a hard disk (called a fixed disk by IBM), a nonremovable 5¼-inch device that is sealed into its drive.

Disk drive   The device used to read and write data on floppy disks and hard disks. A head moves over the spinning disk, rapidly depositing or locating magnetic signals that constitute the data to be written on the disk or already stored there.

Disk operating system (DOS)	The group of programs that control the flow of information into and out of the computer and storage of data on disks. The most widely used DOS for the PC and the XT is PC-DOS.
Hardware	The physical components of a computer system.
Input	Data that is sent into the computer from any of several sources. The principal input device is the keyboard.
Kilobyte	1024 bytes.
Megabyte	1 million bytes.
Memory	The storage area for electronic data within the computer. The memory of the PC and XT consists of random-access memory, or RAM, which is emptied each time the computer is turned off, and read-only memory, or ROM, which remains intact when the computer is turned off.
Microprocessor	The central processing unit, or CPU. The PC and the XT use the Intel 8088 microprocessor, which is known as a 16-bit microprocessor because it can handle data in groups of 16-bits (2 bytes) at a time. An earlier generation of microcomputers used 8-bit microprocessors, such as the Intel 8080 or the Zilog Z80, which process data in 8-bit groups and thus operate more slowly than 16-bit microprocessors.
Monitor	The display unit of a computer system.
Output	Data that is sent out from the computer to any of several devices, such as a monitor or a printer.
Peripherals	A hardware device that is not integral to the computer. Printers and modems are peripheral devices.
Port	A point within the computer through which data enters and exits. A printer is connected to the computer through one of the two types of ports: parallel or serial.
Program	A set of instructions designed for a specific computer use.
Software	The collective term for programs.
System Unit	The component of the PC or the XT that contains the motherboard, the expansion slots, and one or more disk drives.

CHAPTER TWO

How Much Memory Is Enough?

One of the best analogies to help explain the concept of computer memory is the chalkboard. Imagine a chalkboard: a clean slate of black or green onto which you can write or draw all kinds of things. Before putting anything on that board, subdivide the writing area by drawing thousands of boxes with permanent chalk or paint. Each box is large enough to contain only one written character, such as the number 4 or the letter C. Each box is numbered consecutively. Although the number doesn't actually appear in the box, it is associated with that box. The number is essentially an address for that box. Similarly, a computer's memory can be thought of as being divided into many boxes that hold information, each with an identifying address.

Permanent Memory

A personal computer has two kinds of memory: permanent and temporary. Permanent memory comes from the factory, with characters already written in the boxes in the same kind of permanent paint as the outlines of the boxes themselves. The characters in the boxes make up the instructions that the computer follows to read information you type on the keyboard, to display letters and numbers on the monitor, and to perform dozens of basic functions you may not be directly aware of.

When you turn on the computer, the 8088 microprocessor first looks to the permanent memory for instructions; in other words, it "reads" the characters that were written into those boxes at the factory. Permanent memory, called *read-only memory,* or *ROM,* cannot be altered by the computer operator.

A large amount of ROM doesn't necessarily make a "powerful" computer. A lot of what may be contained in one computer's ROM is automatically loaded into another computer from a disk when running a program. Some computers, most notably the IBM PC, include portions of the BASIC programming language in ROM, while others keep the language entirely on disk. Neither method is particularly superior to the other.

But a novice may not be able to judge the quality or the usefulness of ROM content. There isn't an adequate nontechnical test that determines which ROM is better in two computers. A poorly programmed ROM of any size will reveal its weaknesses in the day-to-day operation of the computer. For example, one computer model may have lightning-quick reflexes in retrieving information from a disk, while another is obviously sluggish. In Chapter 12, you'll learn how to determine ROM program differences among PC-compatible computers.

Temporary Memory
Return to the chalkboard analogy to understand the other important kind of memory: *random-access memory,* or *RAM.* With this kind of memory, the chalkboard has a permanent grid painted on it, each box with a different address, but the boxes are blank.

Let's say you're using the computer to write a memo. Every time you press a key on the keyboard—a letter, a number, a punctuation symbol, or a space—that character is placed in one of the boxes on the chalkboard. Inside the computer, the characters are converted to a notation that the computer understands better, which is essentially the "on" and "off" pulses described previously.

In computer terminology, each character or box on the chalkboard is 1 byte. If you type a total of 1024 keystrokes, you will fill precisely 1K of memory with characters. (Even though the prefix *kilo-* should mean 1000, a quirk of computer math makes the outcome 1024, which is close enough to 1000 for convenient reference.)

As with a chalkboard, the contents of a box in the computer's RAM can be erased or changed. Whatever was last written in a box stays there as long as power is supplied to the computer (if you don't erase it yourself). However, once the power is turned off, the contents of the RAM boxes are erased, as if someone took a wet sponge and wiped the chalkboard clean. If that happens, there is no way to reconstruct the information in the boxes without writing the characters into each box from scratch. You can save the information in RAM, however, by storing it on a floppy disk or another storage device. (Chapters 3 and 4 discuss floppy disks and hard disks, the primary storage devices for PC-standard computers.)

Bits and Bytes

One brief lesson in memory terminology is needed before we get to the important, practical questions in considering system memory. It has to do with bits. You'll recall that a character takes up 1 byte of memory, and that each box's address is the location of 1 byte. Just as a molecule can be split into atoms, however, a byte consists of smaller chunks of information, called *bits*. In fact, the circuits inside the computer process information at the bit level (the "on" and "off" signals represented by 1 and 0, respectively). A stream of 8 bits of information makes up one character.

The chips that make up RAM and ROM store information in bit form, even though the computer system as a whole keeps track of the bits in groups of eight. Memory chips are described with terminology such as 8K, 16K, and 64K chips, but because the K denomination for memory chips stands for kilobits (not kilobytes), it actually takes multiples of eight chips to make up the full complement of memory (since 8 bits make up 1 byte).

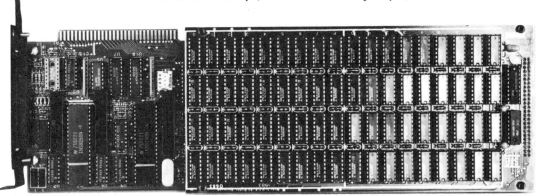

Figure 2.1 *A plug-in memory board. The memory chips occupy about 60 percent of the board's surface (on the right side of the board).*

When you see plug-in memory boards for the PC and the XT, you may be surprised to see so many chips on the boards (see Figure 2.1). Remember that for every 64K (kilobytes) of RAM, you need nine 64K (kilobits) chips (eight for the information and one for an error-checking system built into the computer). A 256K RAM board needs a total of 36 such chips; a 512K RAM board needs 72. (Although the distinction between kilobits and kilobytes has been made here, kilobytes is more commonly used. Therefore, *K* represents kilobytes throughout this book.)

What Goes into Memory

It may be difficult for first-time computer buyers to understand why PC-standard computers seem to have memory capacities rated in staggering amounts compared with machines like the Apple IIe or the Commodore 64. What does anyone do with all that memory?

Programs purchased on floppy disks must be copied (or "loaded") into the computer's memory to operate. A program on a disk contains the instructions that turn the PC into a machine capable of word processing or spreadsheet calculations. When you put a floppy disk into the disk drive and begin the loading procedure, a copy of these instructions is transferred from the disk into RAM.

As noted previously, IBM PC-standard computers are capable of handling larger quantities of memory than popular 8-bit computers. Of the total 1 megabyte of memory possible, only 640K is available as RAM without having to perform special tricks. The balance is reserved for operating parts of the computer system, such as the monitor and ROM.

Programmers have taken advantage of increased memory capacity by designing complex software. It is not uncommon to find single program modules in excess of 100K being loaded into RAM. As programmers continue to design applications to rival those used in more expensive systems, such as minicomputers and mainframes, the trend toward larger program modules will continue.

One of the by-products of these powerful programs and large amounts of RAM is that they can manipulate large amounts of information. Instead of having to load small sections of data from individual disks and working on them in a piecemeal fashion, you can have a data base management program rapidly sort and cross-reference large numbers of records in RAM. Electronic spreadsheets can reach dimensions never before attainable on a personal computer, including not only two-dimensional rows and columns of data but a third dimension for multiple worksheets. Word processing programs can keep large documents in memory and swap blocks of text back and forth without wasting the time normally needed to read and write information from a disk. Most programs that work with large amounts of active data accommodate additional memory dynamically—they can make use of more workspace when you add more RAM to the computer.

Even if a program does not require a large amount of memory, extra RAM in your PC can still be put to use. Depending on your computer and its memory capacity, you can fool your computer into thinking that it has an additional floppy disk drive for data storage, when in reality the drive consists entirely of RAM. This method of turning RAM into an electronic disk drive has many different names, the most common of which are *disk emulator, RAM disk,* and *electronic disk.*

In some situations, using an electronic disk is a smart move. One such situation is using a program that has a number of modules, so that the computer must frequently pause and retrieve information from a floppy disk. Because access time to a floppy disk is generally slow compared with the computational speed within RAM, waiting for the disk drive to finish its reading chore may become distracting or downright annoying. To alleviate this problem, you can transfer all modules of the program to an electronic disk. When you run the program, instead of waiting for a disk drive's motor to spin and the drive to find the program segment on the disk, the computer retrieves the information from RAM in an instant.

You will probably also want to use an electronic disk with programs that frequently read and write data on a storage disk (a disk containing your work) during program execution. A data base management program, for example, may keep very little of an electronic file in RAM. Whenever you want to view, search, or sort through your records, the program performs multiple readings and writings from the disk. With a large file, the waiting time for all the disk maneuvers could be excessive.

You must take one precaution with electronic disks, however. If you make additions or changes in data on an electronic disk, you must copy them to the floppy disk before turning off the computer. Otherwise, like an eraser wiping a chalkboard clean, your work will disappear when the computer is turned off.

One last way to effectively utilize memory involves printing. Many memory expansion boards let you assign a segment of memory for a process known as *print spooling.* Essentially, this operation uses the designated memory to hold information for use by a printer, freeing the main RAM and microprocessor for other tasks.

Electronic disks and print spooling programs are often provided as part of software packages sold with memory expansion boards. The precise methods and commands that initiate these functions vary from manufacturer to manufacturer, but all operate in a similar manner.

System Unit Memory

The System Board contains dozens of integrated circuits (ICs), which look like black plastic or ceramic rectangles with lots of connector pins going into the circuit board. Along the left side of the System Board (as you face the computer) are four rows of nine IC sockets. The standard PC configuration has one row already filled with chips from the factory. These are the RAM chips, where information you type or load into memory is first stored. Each row of RAM chips represents 64K of memory.

The first-generation PC (before the introduction of the XT) had only 16K of RAM installed. At that time, IBM was using smaller capacity 16K RAM chips on the System Board. Four rows of 16K RAM chips brought the maximum on-board memory to 64K. But IBM soon discovered that many customers were buying a "bare" 16K machine and filling the remaining sockets with less expensive 16K RAM chips manufactured by outside suppliers. As a result, IBM discontinued sending 16K System Units to dealers (although they remained available on special order) and began supplying fully loaded 64K ones.

When IBM's engineers created the XT, they designed the System Board for 64K RAM chips. This change was also instituted on the PC. If you consider buying a used PC, be sure to inspect the System Board to determine whether it is the older or newer version, because you will want maximum flexibility in adding RAM.

One way to distinguish the older System Boards from the newer ones is to look on the board along its left edge next to the RAM sockets. On the newer version, you will see numbers printed on the board that signify the amounts of RAM in each row of chips. Starting from the front of the computer, the numbering goes 64K, 128K, 192K, and 256K. If these numbers are not present, the system is probably an older version.

Installing Additional Memory

Today, the standard PC comes equipped with 64K of RAM, and the XT comes with 128K. Both machines have vacant RAM sockets on the System Board for a total capacity of 256K RAM. All sockets on the PC's System Board must be filled before more memory can be added to this machine, although you can add a plug-in memory board to the XT without filling all the sockets on its System Board.

To get more than 256K, you will have to install a plug-in board in one of the expansion slots. Memory expansion boards come in two varieties. One is devoted solely to memory expansion (this is not recommended), and the other combines additional memory with one or more other functions, such as a serial adapter, a game controller connector, or a built-in clock/calendar. This type of multifunction board is recommended, because it allows you to avoid devoting an expansion slot exclusively to memory.

Although you can buy memory boards with as little as 32K of RAM, be sure that the memory expansion board you have can accommodate at least 256K. You don't have to buy a fully loaded memory board, however; you can install additional RAM chips as your memory requirements increase.

Because the price of fully loaded memory and multifunction boards has dropped significantly, it may not be particularly advantageous to wait until you need extra RAM before buying chip sets. Adding chips may seem like a relatively simple task, especially because they appear to plug into sockets on the board, but only a careful hand can insert them correctly without bending the pins. (Most electronics stores sell a tool that can help with chip installation.) In dry climates, particularly during the winter months, static electricity can play havoc with the chips as you handle them. A tiny spark of static electricity can wipe out a chip in a flash. If you're unsure of your dexterity, you should probably either leave chip installation to a dealer or buy a fully loaded memory board.

When you install additional memory in the PC, you'll have to set a series of small switches on the System Board, and possibly on the memory board if you use one. The System Board switch settings on the PC tell the system the total amount of memory you have installed. In the XT, the switch settings control only the memory installed on the System Board. (See the IBM *Guide to Operations* for more information on setting switches.)

A memory board may have other switches that tell the computer where to find the additional memory. Some boards are preset to eliminate the need for setting switches, unless you are installing more than one memory board. Most memory expansion boards come with a manual describing how the switches must be set.

How Much Memory for You?
Now you have to figure out how much RAM you will need to have in your PC. For running entertainment and educational software, 64K of RAM should be adequate, because most software in these categories is designed to work with this standard memory amount.

For professional applications, you should have at least enough memory to handle the popular programs for spreadsheets, word processing, and data base management. Most programs in these areas require or work best with a minimum of 128K of RAM. Of course, if you end up buying the XT, you will already have that much RAM.

For programs that let you devote segments of RAM on electronic disk, you should be prepared to have enough total memory to accommodate both your applications program (perhaps 128K) and the equivalent of a 320K electronic disk, although for most applications you can get by with less electronic disk space at first. A 256K PC or XT with a 192K expansion board will support most applications adequately.

On some of the newer memory expansion boards, you can piggyback an additional memory component (a smaller board), which can bring the total RAM inside your PC to 1 megabyte. Although you may not think you will ever need so much memory, several powerful programs use 512K just for program operation and temporary information storage. If you also want electronic disks and print spooling, you will definitely need more than 512K.

It's best to equip your PC with a minimum of 128K, and preferably 256K, which will bring your computer's memory to the System Board's maximum 256K of RAM. Since eventually you probably will want other functions that are available on multifunction memory expansion boards, buy one that can hold at least 256K of RAM, even if you buy it without all the RAM chips installed. (Note, though, that you must fill all sockets on the PC's System Board before adding a plug-in memory board.) If, however, your primary purpose for buying the PC—especially the XT model—is to use the more sophisticated applications such as *1-2-3* (Lotus), *MBA* (Context), or *Visi On* (VisiCorp), you should have 256K to run *1-2-3* and *MBA* and 512K to run *Visi On*. For the most effective long-range planning, choose a multifunction memory expansion board that lets you add an extra memory board later (without taking up a second slot), for a total of 1 megabyte of RAM.

Tips for Adding Memory

■ In general, memory chips should be installed in all sockets on the computer's system board before a plug-in memory board is added.

■ If your plan to install memory chips (on the system board or on a plug-in memory board) yourself, the task will be much easier if you purchase a chip installation kit at an electronics store. The kit contains tools that are designed for installing and removing chips from sockets on a circuit board.

■ You will make the most efficient use of your computer's expansion slots if you choose a multifunction board. You can purchase a memory board that also has a parallel port (for a printer) and one or two serial ports (for a modem, a mouse, or another peripheral).

■ Whatever amount of memory you decide to add to your computer, purchase a board that is designed to handle even more memory. Most popular plug-in boards are designed to hold 256K of RAM, although you can usually buy one that has as little as 64K of memory installed, and add more chips later. Some of the boards supplied with 256K can be upgraded to 512K. If you choose an expandable memory board, be sure that it contains all the sockets, so that all you have to do is add chips.

■ If you plan to use part of the computer's memory as an electronic disk or if you use integrated or highly complex applications programs, your system should have at least 256K of memory, and preferably more.

CHAPTER THREE

Floppy Disks and Drives

If you've used inexpensive home computers, you've probably had to wrestle with a cassette player to load prerecorded programs or store information. Being able to transfer computer data from the computer to tape probably seemed adequate at first. Information was transferred at speeds of 500 to more than 1800 bits per second (50 to 180 characters per second), depending on the system you used.

But working with cassette tapes quickly loses its appeal. Loading programs from tape is not always successful, and the volume and tone controls of the cassette recorder must be set just right to ensure that data is loaded. The wait for the tape to load or store data can seem interminable. And the larger the program, the longer the loading time.

Fortunately, the technologies and devices for storing data have advanced well beyond the cassette recorder in both speed and efficiency. The principal storage medium for PC-standard computers is the floppy disk and disk drive, and even more advanced devices are coming into use as well.

Although cassettes are seldom used with it, the PC is built to accept a cassette player for use as a storage device. All you need is the IBM cable that connects the computer and the cassette recorder, and the recorder and the tapes. But because few PCs are sold without at least one disk drive, little cassette software is available for the PC. And since you will likely be running sophisticated programs involving considerable amounts of data for storage, a cassette player, even as a beginning mass storage device, is not recommended.

The Disk

Imagine removing the tape from inside a cassette and laying strips of it down in circles on a flat platter like a record. Instead of having the tape move across a stationary tape head (as in a recorder), the tape platter spins and the tape head moves from strip to strip. This is a crude but accurate representation of a floppy disk and a disk drive. The medium is magnetic, like magnetic tape, except that the design of the disk surface and the drive's read/write head permits an enormous amount of information to be stored in a much smaller area than on a corresponding area of tape.

If you look closely at a disk, you will see that the magnetic medium—the actual disk—is housed in a cardboard jacket with several holes exposing the disk surface where the data is stored (see Fig-

Figure 3.1 *A 5¼-inch floppy disk, the type used in the PC and most PC-standard computers.*

ure 3.1). The jacket protects the disk's surface from being touched or exposed to dust and dirt. Oils from even freshly washed hands can stick to the disk's surface, as can dust or smoke particles. To a disk drive's read/write head, a cat hair can seem like a fallen tree.

Disks are constructed so that you can hold them by the jacket when you are inserting or removing them from a disk drive. When they are not being used, they should always be stored in the paper envelopes supplied with them.

Although "floppy" disks are indeed pliable, if they are creased or bent, the data on them and even the disk drive's read/write head may be damaged. Instead of storing disks in the cardboard box they are sold in, store them in a hard plastic box—either a "library" box, which holds about 10 disks, or a "flip file," which holds from 25 to 100 or more disks for quick access. To keep dust and other foreign matter away from the disks, the plastic containers should be kept closed, except when you are removing or replacing a disk.

Caring for disks requires a number of other caveats, including using only felt-tip pens to label them (never pencils or ball-point pens), and protecting them from temperature extremes and exposure to magnetic fields such as the bell in a telephone. The illustrations and the notes on the back of most disk envelopes provide a useful quick reference to disk care.

Disk Sizes

Floppy disks currently come in three diameters: 8, 5¼, and 3½ inches. The first two sizes are established industry standards and have been used for years (the 8-inch disk preceded the 5¼-inch version). But because the 3½-inch disk is not yet a standard, other manufacturers are offering disks that range from 3¼ to 4 inches in diameter. Since the 8-inch disk was the original standard, the 5¼-inch disk is sometimes called a minifloppy and the 3½-inch disk a microfloppy. A rule of thumb used to be that the larger the disk diameter, the greater the data capacity, but some computers now can store more data on a 3½-inch disk than others can put on a 5¼-inch floppy.

The 8-inch disk does not play a role in PC-standard computers. Most 8-inch disks are used in business minicomputers and computers that use the CP/M operating system. One advantage of the 8-inch disk (aside from its large storage capacity) is that the computer industry standardized not only the size of the disk but also the manner in which data should be mapped out, or formatted, on the disk. An 8-inch CP/M-compatible disk is readable on any CP/M system that has an 8-inch disk drive. Such compatibility does not exist with all the newer, smaller disks.

Most personal computers today—including the PC—use 5¼-inch disks. But there is little in the way of a format standard among the various computers, even among computers using the same operating system. This problem is less of a factor, however, with PC-standard computers, because most manufacturers want their machines to be as compatible as possible with the PC.

The 3½-inch disks are even less standardized than the 5¼-inch disks. In PC-standard computers, these microfloppy disks are currently limited to portable computers such as the Gavilan, which is purportedly PC compatible. The microfloppy disks present special problems, however (see Chapter 12).

The Disk Drive

Just as the cassette needs a recorder to save and load data, a disk needs a special device called a disk drive. It is a complicated device, and unlike most of the PC, it is largely electromechanical. A motor spins the disk at a speed of 300 revolutions per minute (rpm), compared with 33 rpm of a record album, for example. Another motor adjusts the read/write head to precise locations over the disk surface through the long oval opening in the disk jacket.

The read/write head is the most sensitive part of the disk drive. It must be specially aligned to locate and store information in precise locations on the spinning disk. If properly aligned, a disk drive needs little maintenance (unless the computer in which it is installed takes the bumps and bruises of a portable computer).

When a disk drive is spinning, a red light on the drive's front panel shines. When the light is on, you should not open the disk drive door. Disturbing a drive when it is transferring data can damage the data stored on that disk.

PC-standard disk drives come in different heights. The drive supplied on the PC is the standard height; other machines, such as the Eagle PC, the IBM Portable PC, and other portables, use half-height disk drives. The half-height drives represent an advance over the standard disk drives, because the mechanical parts in the drive have been redesigned so that the entire package fits in half the space of a standard drive. (This smaller size has no bearing on the amount of data that can be stored on a disk.)

In portable computers, half-height disk drives squeeze a lot of mass storage capacity into a small cabinet. And in desktop PC compatibles, the half-height drives enable designers to create a lower profile machine. The PCjr, for example, uses a half-height drive.

There are two kinds of disk drive doors in PC-standard computers. One is the latch-type door that you either lift up to open and push down to close (as in the PC), or flip from side to side (as in the

Compaq). The other kind employs an elongated knob that rotates one-quarter turn to lock a disk in the drive. When it is in the vertical position, the door is closed, dutifully preventing you from removing or inserting a disk. To open it, you just turn the knob to one side.

Disk Storage Capacities
There are single- and double-sided disks. Although both sides of all disks are coated with the magnetic medium, only one side of a single-sided disk is tested and guaranteed to store data.

A single-sided disk drive on a PC or an XT can store as much as 180K of programs or information. (This kilobyte unit measurement is identical to the kilobyte unit previously discussed relative to RAM.) In other words, a single-sided disk has the capacity to store one-and-a-half times as much information as a PC with 128K of RAM.

Early versions of the PC's principal operating system, PC-DOS, known by chronological release numbers 1.00 and 1.10, limited single-sided disk storage to 160K. Later versions, DOS 2.00 and 2.10, wedge a little more data onto a disk, bringing the total to 180K. Fortunately, DOS 2.00 and more recent versions can use disks formatted with DOS 1.10.

As their name implies, double-sided disks can store information on boths sides of the disk. Both sides are given identical quality control checks at the time of manufacture, assuring reliable disk storage. To use a double-sided disk, you need a double-sided disk drive, which has two sets of read/write heads, one for each side of the disk.

Storage capacity of double-sided disks is, as you'd expect, double that of single-sided disks. In DOS 2.00 or later versions, you can store up to 360K on one disk (320K with DOS 1.10). Because blank, double-sided disks cost only slightly more than single-sided disks (about 10 to 15 percent more depending on the brand), they are more economical. Although you can use single-sided disks in a double-sided drive, the second side of the disk has not been tested and is not guaranteed. Many people use single-sided disks in double-sided drives, even though the disks' second sides have not been tested. Because PC-DOS will locate any bad areas on a disk and mark them as unusable during disk formatting, using single-sided disks is not especially risky.

Single- or Double-Sided?
The many choices available in disk drive storage on the IBM PC (one or two drives, single- or double-sided) can seem rather confusing at

first. In an effort to save money when assembling a PC system, many owners select single-sided disk drives—usually two. A single-sided drive reads and writes data on only one side of a disk.

Buying a PC-standard computer that has single-sided disk drives is shortsighted. At first you may think that 180K of storage per disk is plenty, but after a month or two of filling up disks, you are likely to find single-sided disks piling up around your computer.

Although most PC software is manufactured on single-sided disks, manufacturers do so for the convenience of PC owners who have the smaller capacity drives, because double-sided drives can read single-sided disks. But because complex programs often need more than 160K or 180K of disk space, they have to be offered in several modules on more than one disk. If you run such a program as delivered, you'll find yourself swapping program disks rather often. But with a double-sided disk drive, you can put all the modules on one disk and eliminate disk swapping altogether. You can also put two or more related programs such as word processing and a spelling checker on one disk. You'll be able to move among applications without losing time fumbling for disks.

If you start with a single-sided disk drive and later decide that you need a double-sided drive, you will lose in the expansion sweepstakes. Your initial single-sided disk drive investment will have dwindled to practically nothing, and you'll have to pay full price for the double-sided drives. When you add up all the dollars spent on upgrading your drives, you'll end up paying about one-and-a-half times the cost of buying double-sided drives in the first place. Some dealers offer liberal trade-ins on single-sided disk drives, but such dealers are rare, so don't count on it.

One Drive or Two?

Another important choice is whether to buy one or two disk drives for the standard PC (the XT comes with one floppy and one hard disk, leaving no room for an extra drive in the System Unit). Because many PC compatibles come equipped with two double-sided drives, decisions about disk drives won't be necessary for those machines. For the PC, however, the question is a valid one.

Although many programs are advertised as operating successfully with one disk drive, the advertisements fail to warn that using a single drive can be quite a nuisance. Most business-oriented software includes at least one program disk and either recommends or requires that your work be stored on a separate disk. Sometimes the entire program will load into the computer at the beginning of the session. If this is the case, the operating sequence is as follows: insert the program disk into the drive; start the computer; when the program is loaded, remove the program disk from the drive; and insert the storage disk into the drive. That doesn't sound so bad, does it? But with other programs, the program disk is accessed often to load separate modules. If that's the case, you may spend a lot of time swapping disks in a single disk drive.

Setting up your programs to run on the PC often requires a one-time installation procedure (discussed in detail in Chapter 9). Depending on the program, the process will be simplified if you have two disk drives. If you buy only one disk drive initially, adding a second drive won't require you to sell one at a loss or discard it. But your dealer may give you a better package price if you have two disk drives installed in your original system. For both savings and efficiency, a two-drive system is a wise investment.

CHAPTER FOUR

Hard Disk Drives

Hard disk drives are the same size as standard 5¼-inch floppy disk drives, but they offer the PC owner as much mass storage as room-sized mainframe computers offered corporate giants during the 1970s. Hard disk storage capacities are measured in millions of bytes—megabytes—rather than thousands of bytes. As you might imagine, cramming that much data into such a small space enables personal computers to take on applications never before possible.

These drives are called hard disks, because the actual storage medium is a rigid, circular platter or series of platters stacked on top of one another with about a ¼-inch gap between them. There are two types of hard disks: fixed and removable. Fixed disks (which IBM uses in the XT) have platters mounted permanently inside the disk drive enclosure (see Figure 4.1), while hard disk drives that have removable media let the user insert and remove cartridges containing the actual disks (see Figure 4.2).

The hard disk platters of both types of drives are coated with a metallic oxide substance that is much finer than the oxide on floppy disks. During operation, the disks spin at 3600 rpm, compared with a floppy disk's 300 rpm. In addition, data is much more densely packed on a hard disk than on a floppy.

Although a hard disk's read/write heads transfer data to and from the disks as on a floppy drive, they operate on a different principle. Instead of touching the surface of the disk, each head is sus-

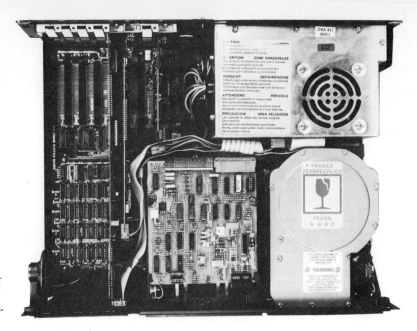

Figure 4.1 *The interior of the XT, showing the hard disk in the lower right corner of the photograph.*

pended over the surface by a microscopic cushion of air created by the whirring platters. As the disks spin, the heads move back and forth above the disk to access a particular track and sector.

Although dust can be a problem with floppy disks, it is even more of a threat to a hard disk. That's why hard disk systems have the recording medium and heads housed in a sealed compartment, minimizing the possibility that contamination could reach the disk's surface.

Because maintaining the gap between head and platter is essential to protect the head from scratching the platter, a hard disk system must be carefully engineered to withstand shock, such as that of a heavy book falling on the System Unit. Hard disks in portable computers must be especially well protected from shock. But no matter how well designed a particular disk system may be, never move a computer while the disk drive is in operation.

Performance and Capacities

Although the read/write speed of hard disks varies from manufacturer to manufacturer, a hard disk's data transfer speed falls somewhere between a floppy disk's and an electronic disk's. Hard disks don't have the instantaneous response of electronic disks, but they are considerably faster than floppy disks. For example, the data transfer rate of the PC's floppy disk drive is rated at 250 kilobits per

Figure 4.2 *A cartridge hard disk in its own cabinet, and a disk cartridge (at lower right).*

second, whereas the XT's fixed disk drive is rated at 5 megabits per second—20 times faster than the floppy disk drive.

IBM's standard hard disk is a 10-megabyte fixed disk. It offers 10,000K of storage—slightly less than the storage provided by 28 double-sided floppy disks. Independent suppliers of hard disks offer several capacities of hard disk storage, ranging from 5 megabytes to more than 72 megabytes. Ten-megabyte hard disks are generally the most popular, especially in terms of cost (they generally cost between $1000 and $2500).

How to Use a Hard Disk
To novices, 10 million bytes of storage capacity is enough to boggle the mind. You might even think that a hard disk can replace floppy disks altogether, and that you can store all your word processing documents, spreadsheets, and your company's entire mailing list on the hard disk. Wrong! You must plan hard disk usage carefully; otherwise, you run the risk of quickly outgrowing any hard disk you buy for the PC. Like a garage cluttered with useless articles, a hard disk can rapidly fill up if you treat it as a repository for everything your computer creates.

PC-DOS versions 2.00 and higher provide numerous utility programs to help you organize the large amounts of information that can stack up on a hard disk. Most importantly, you can group related files into subdirectories to help you keep track of files in an organized manner. The process is similar to keeping related file folders in a single cabinet drawer and labeling the drawer with a descriptive title. For example, you can keep your spreadsheet data in a subdirectory called Spread. To see what spreadsheet files you have stored on the hard disk, you would type in a command that displays the contents of the Spread subdirectory, instead of having to view a directory of all the files stored on the hard disk.

A hard disk should contain only those programs and data files that you use on a regular basis or are using in a current job. For example, software that you use routinely—such as word processing, data base management, graphics, and telecommunications—should be kept on the hard disk for easy access. If you keep seldom-used programs on floppy disks and load them when you need them, you will be able to conserve hard disk space.

The kind of data you keep on a hard disk will vary accordin to the applications you use. If you often assemble word processing documents from boilerplate text, as with contracts or customer reply letters, you might keep those stock letters and text on the hard disk so they are readily accessible. For spreadsheets or other financial software, any information that you use repeatedly, such as spreadsheet templates, should also be readily available on the hard disk. Data base files, such as mailing lists, inventories, personnel records, and other frequently accessed information, should also be kept handy—on the hard disk.

Information used infrequently or that merely serves as a record or a backup copy of data should be transferred to floppy disks (or another storage medium) and kept in a safe place. Think of the hard disk as a cabinet of current files that you open regularly to retrieve or update information. When you begin using some of those files less frequently, pull them out of the file cabinet and store them in labeled storage boxes. Consider the hard disk your current file cabinet and your floppy disks the storage boxes deserving safekeeping.

Backing Up Hard Disks

Although a hard disk is generally a reliable storage medium, there is the possibility that something could go wrong—and spell disaster. If any problem is going to befall a floppy disk drive, it will usually affect only a small portion of the disk, making one or two sectors (of 512 bytes each) unavailable to the read/write heads. The most information that can be lost in a floppy disk system is the amount stored on a single disk (360K for a double-sided disk). On a hard disk, however, the potential for disaster is more substantial—the contents of an entire 10- or 20-megabyte disk drive could be wiped out.

The most disastrous loss of information comes from a "head crash," in which a read/write head in the drive somehow comes into contact with one of the platters. Even though only a portion of the disk will be physically damaged, all the data and the programs stored on the disk will be lost if you must reformat the disk to reposition the head.

Fortunately, there is a way to guard against losing your data—making backup copies of the hard disk's data onto floppy disks. If your files are extensive, this can be a time-consuming process requiring copying information to several different floppies at the end of each work session. But those efforts won't be nearly as difficult as reconstructing dozens of files from scratch if you lose a hard disk's contents. PC-DOS 2.00 and later releases have built-in commands that assist in backing up hard disk files on floppy disks. If you have the patience to learn the fine points of DOS commands, you can even have the computer perform the backup operation automatically each time you've finished a work session.

Some independent hard disk manufacturers offer other methods of backing up hard disks. The Corvus Systems hard disk, for example, lets you add an adapter that transfers data to a videotape recorder at greater speeds than transfers to floppy disks. Another type of backup system features a built-in tape cartridge (sometimes called a stringy floppy), which performs automatic transfer upon typed commands. The tape cartridge is removable and can be stored in a safe place when not being used.

Although a hard disk offers mass storage power and flexibility, with those extra features comes the responsibility of performing periodic "maintenance." This kind of disk maintenance is one of the things that data processing managers in corporate computer rooms get paid to do. Failure to monitor your disk usage may result in a hopelessly jumbled and practically useless hodgepodge of files. Be prepared for the care that a hard disk requires.

PC Hard Disk Options
Let's take a look at the hard disk choices you have for the standard PC. (The XT is a special case that is discussed later in this chapter.)

The PC's built-in power supply was designed primarily for two floppy disk drives. Rated at 63.5 watts (compared with the XT's 130 watts), the PC's power supply cannot deliver enough current to supply power for a built-in hard disk in addition to all the expansion cards drawing current through the expansion slots. For this reason, the fixed disk that IBM sells for its XT and two models of the Expansion Units will not work inside the PC System Unit.

Hard disks are sold in two configurations, internal and external. Perhaps the most popular type integrates the hard disk into the

System Unit, replacing the floppy disk drive on the right. What you can't see in the ads, however, is that most of these drives require external power supplies. Designers of a few of them have fashioned a power supply box that attaches to the rear panel of the System Unit with a custom bracket. This design increases the overall depth of the System Unit—a dimension already rather large for many desks. Other manufacturers offer a completely separate power supply box that can be positioned next to, behind, or on the floor beneath the System Unit. Avoid a hard disk that draws power from the standard PC power supply; it could overtax the power supply of a PC containing several expansion boards and cause overheating inside the System Unit.

Another alternative to the internal hard disk is a hard disk subsystem housed in a separate box connected via a cable to a hard disk controller board inside the PC. For PC owners who have become accustomed to using two floppy disk drives, the subsystem may be a worthwhile addition when they find that they need a hard disk. They may also have used software on their two-drive PCs that cannot be copied or used on a hard disk without costly software upgrades. In this situation, they may need both floppy disk drives to run those programs.

Just because a program disk can be copied doesn't mean that it will be fully functional on a hard disk. With Version 3.2 of *WordStar* (MicroPro's word processing program), for example, if you have the program on a hard disk and use one of the floppy disk drives for automatic document storage, the program has a built-in routine that searches the floppy disk in drive A every time the computer needs further instructions from the program. Since the program is not in drive A but is on the hard disk, which is usually drive C, *WordStar* will be stumped and display an error message. (Version 3.3 of *WordStar* has corrected this problem, but it may still exist for other programs.) If you are buying a PC and software now, however, most of the software you will be adding to your system should be compatible with DOS version 2.00 and higher, and have some kind of hard disk support for internal or external hard disk drives.

If you prefer to stay with IBM, you can purchase the Expansion Unit for the PC, but that is an expensive option. It looks just like the System Unit but contains eight expansion slots and has room for two disk drives. With floppies in the System Unit, you can use the Expansion Unit for up to two fixed disk drives.

An important point to remember about adding a hard disk to the PC is that in addition to the floppy disk drive controller board required for the floppies, you need room for a hard disk drive controller board in the PC's limited slots. It is unlikely that you will find a multifunction board containing a hard disk controller, because every manufacturer's hard disk board is different. If you plan to buy a PC that has two floppy drives and add a hard disk later, reserve room in your expansion slots for the hard disk controller.

XT Hard Disk Options

Standard equipment on the XT includes a 10-megabyte fixed disk drive and one double-sided floppy disk drive. You may wonder why you can't put two hard disk drives in the System Unit and have a massive 20 megabytes of storage. Remember that the software you buy is always supplied on floppy disks (except, of course, the small number of programs available on telecommunications bulletin boards). You will need at least one floppy disk drive to get your programs into the computer and copied to the hard disk. You will also want a convenient way to back up your hard disk files. A floppy disk is essential and one of the most economical backup tools.

You can add more than one hard disk to the XT using the IBM Expansion Unit, but not without some maneuvering. To assure the integrity of data transfers from multiple hard disks to the System Board in the System Unit, IBM advises keeping both fixed disk drives in the same cabinet. Because the floppy disk drive controller board must be mounted in the main System Unit, the Expansion Unit is the only candidate for housing both fixed disks.

Converting an XT to a two-hard-disk XT/Expansion Unit requires shuffling the original hard disk and hard disk controller over to the Expansion Unit. This is not a difficult job, but it may be awkward for an XT owner who is nervous about digging inside a $5000 computer. Cabling is simplified greatly by the multiple-pin connectors and cable harnesses designed into the floppy and fixed disk subassemblies, adapters, and power supplies. (Complete instructions are provided with the Expansion Unit.) Once the transfer is completed, you will have room in the System Unit for a second floppy disk drive. If you don't want to add that drive, you can use one of the drive well covers from the Expansion Unit to cover the gap in the System Unit.

Is One Floppy Disk Drive Enough?

If you customarily use two floppy disk drives, you may feel a bit squeamish about having only one, even with a hard disk at your disposal. Provided that all the necessary software can be copied onto the hard disk, one of the major reasons for having two floppies (one for the program disk and another for data storage) is virtually eliminated.

Two disk drives come in handy when you are conducting file maintenance chores for your floppy disks (when you need to copy program or data files from one floppy disk to another). With only one drive, copying files can be a time-consuming chore, full of pit-falls as you follow often confusing on-screen instructions for swapping disks in a single drive.

One way to copy disks if you have only one disk drive is to use an electronic disk (and expanded RAM). Instead of copying files from one disk directly to another, you copy the contents of the original floppy disk to the electronic disk, then copy the contents of the electronic disk to another floppy disk. This process is much faster for a disk full of files, but it is not as automatic or as fast as it is with two floppy drives. The subdirectory structures available in DOS 2.00 also provide an easy way to copy disks if you have one floppy drive and a hard disk. You can load the contents of a floppy into one subdirectory on the hard disk, then copy it to another floppy.

Hard Disk Recommendations
Deciding whether to buy a hard disk is perhaps one of the most difficult decisions you are likely to encounter when assembling your PC system. If you have an immediate need for a hard disk (because of known storage requirements or because you want to use programs such as *Visi On* that require a hard disk), the XT is a cost-effective machine to start out with. Not only is the XT a reasonably well-priced package (compared with upgrading a PC), but it keeps the hard disk self-contained (no external power supply needed) and offers extra expansion slots for further system growth.

If hard disk storage is something that you can put off, you may want to start with the standard PC and two floppy disk drives, and add an external hard disk later. When you're ready to add the hard disk, you will have a number of attractive options available to you, including disk subsystems having 20 or more megabytes of storage and built-in backup mechanisms. The main advantage of waiting for a hard disk is that improving technology and increased popularity will continue to reduce the cost of this practical and efficient mass storage medium. If you have an immediate need for a hard disk, however, don't delay the purchase.

XT owners will always have the occasional problem of having copy-protected software that cannot be copied to the hard disk, obviating one of the main advantages of the hard disk medium. An attractive alternative is to replace the XT's one floppy disk drive with two half-height floppy disk drives. With this combination, you will be ready to handle any software possibilities that come your way. The only problem such an alternative presents is that the drives will not be IBM equipment, which could interfere with warranty or repair arrangements.

Hard Disks and Compatibles

Most PC-compatible computers don't offer as much flexibility as the IBM models when it comes to adding hard disk drives. Models that are equipped with a hard disk (usually with one floppy as well) may not provide the eight expansion slots available in the XT. Expansion beyond the standard equipment may not be possible with these machines.

Of course, a portable computer that is not meant to be the heart of a large data storage system shouldn't need any more than one hard disk. A portable machine with two floppies might be more efficient in any event.

Monitors

Unlike many home computers that display text and color graphics on a TV, the PC and some PC compatibles have as many as four options for displaying computer output on a video screen. In the PC's case, each type of display requires one of IBM's two boards or a similar board from an independent supplier. Thus your monitor selection will affect how efficiently you use the PC's expansion slots.

The four monitor options are: the IBM Monochrome Display, the IBM Color Display or another RGB (red-green-blue) color monitor, a composite color monitor, and a monochrome graphics monitor. And depending on the monitor you select for the PC, you will need either the IBM Monochrome Display Adapter or the Color/Graphics Adapter.

No single type of monitor provides optimum display quality for all varieties of work. In some cases, you will have no alternative but to use two monitors if your applications require both legible text and high-quality graphics. Although choosing the proper monitor may seem confusing, an understanding of how each one works and the kind of work for which it is best suited should help you make an informed selection.

CRT Basics

A computer monitor is often called a CRT, which stands for cathode ray tube. The CRT is the actual picture tube of the monitor, like that in a TV. Its name is derived from its operation: an electron ray, or a beam, generated by an element in the tube called the cathode, is directed against the face of the tube.

Think of the screen as a blank canvas and the electron beam as the artist's brush. In a black-and-white display (or monochrome, which simply means single-color), the brush paints a thin line across the screen, from left to right, starting from the top line. Depending on the picture it is drawing, the brush marks segments of the line with varying shades of gray. After painting one line, the brush paints another directly below it. As each succeeding line is painted, a recognizable picture emerges.

Now imagine that the brush paints each line so fast that it fills an entire canvas with more than 300 lines 30 times every second. That's how fast a standard TV picture is "refreshed" by the electron beam in the CRT. If the patterns of light, dark, and gray change slightly as these lines fill the screen, they produce the illusion of moving objects, just like succeeding frames of motion picture film.

The "canvas" of a CRT is actually a phosphor-coated glass surface. Where the high-voltage electron beam strikes the phosphor, a spot glows. The greater the intensity of the beam at that instant, the brighter the phosphor spot glows. But it can't glow too long, or it could carry over into the next "frame," which may call for it to be dark.

A color monitor operates on the same principles, but with the added complexity of having usually three electron beam guns in the CRT and a more intricate screen phosphor than a monochrome monitor has. Each gun generates an electron beam whose intensity is determined by the amount of red, green, and blue needed to reproduce a particular color shade at any spot on the phosphor screen. The beams are not colored. Instead, each beam is precisely focused to illuminate phosphor of the appropriate color at every spot, or picture element, on the screen. Every picture element consists of a closely spaced group of three phosphor dots that emit red, green, and blue light when struck by their respective electron beams. From a normal viewing distance, the colors at each picture element appear to blend and can recreate the full range of colors.

Another pertinent technical concern is *bandwidth,* a term used in monitor specifications. A bandwidth specification is like the measurement of an opening in a tube through which you are trying to push something. To understand this concept, imagine a paint spray gun (connected by a hose to a gallon of paint) and a wall. The gallon of paint represents the computer, the wall represents the monitor screen, and the hose acts as the circuitry in a monitor that controls the amount of information that can pass to the screen. If the speed at which you sweep the spray gun across the wall—line by line—is constant, the width of the hose will dictate the quality of paint coverage for each sweep. A narrow hose produces spotty coverage and a wide hose solid coverage.

Going one step closer to what happens in a color monitor, let's say that instead of a steady stream of paint moving through the hose, a regulator of some kind at the gallon can sends paint in short spurts in order to create a dot pattern as you sweep the gun across the wall. The regulator sends carefully measured bursts of paint. If the hose is too narrow, the paint needs more time to get through the tube and onto the wall. What is supposed to be a circular dot comes out looking more like an oval—elongated in the direction of the spray gun sweep. By the time you're done sweeping every line of the wall, the dot pattern looks sloppy, as if someone had smeared the paint.

To display letters, numbers, and other text characters on a computer monitor, the "paint" sprayed is a string of bursts from the electron gun that creates rows of "on" and "off" dots on the phosphor screen. For example, look at the number 7 as shown in Figure 5.1. Notice that the top row of the number 7 has 7 dots across, and in the second row there are 4 dots. The remaining rows each have 2 dots, placed strategically to make this row of dots look like a 7. The more characters the computer displays across the screen, the more dots the beam has to paint on every pass.

Figure 5.1 *A graphic representation of the number 7 as displayed on the IBM Monochrome Display, along with the letter* j, *showing the two rows of dots that make up its descender.*

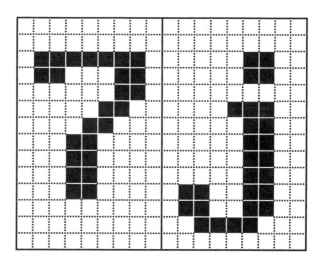

Monitors having insufficient bandwidth to handle output from the computer produce inferior displays, just as paint pushed through a narrow hose is splotchy or blurred. Text, in particular, is adversely affected by a very low bandwidth. The result may be an illegible display that has fuzzy-looking letters blending into one another.

The IBM Monochrome Display and Display Adapter

Probably the most popular of all monitors used with the PC is the IBM Monochrome Display. Intended for text display only, it is the equivalent size of a 12-inch-diagonal TV, but it has a number of unusual properties of its own, especially in concert with the display adapter designed for it.

The IBM Monochrome Display is capable of presenting every character of the PC's character set, an impressive list of letters, numbers, and punctuation marks, and a variety of predefined graphics characters. Each character is formed by a grid, or matrix, of dots in a maximum area of 9 dots horizontally by 14 dots vertically. Letters and numbers are formed within a 7-by-9-dot matrix, plus dots from two additional rows for descenders (the tails on lowercase letters g, j, p, q, and y). Graphics characters, however, can extend to the boundaries of the entire 9-by-14-dot character box.

The Monochrome Display's 7-by-9-dot character is a significant improvement over most other computer displays, including the IBM Color Display, which constructs characters from a 5-by-7-dot matrix (see Figure 5.2). Because the Monochrome Display has 60 percent more dots in the matrix, the resolution of each character is substantially better, and the individual dots are barely visible. In addition, word processing programs frequently take advantage of the Monochrome Display's ability to underline and highlight text the way it would appear on a piece of paper. Of all the monitors for the PC, only this one produces these font enhancements to give you a true representation of your documents.

Several other features of the Monochrome Display come together to produce excellent resolution for these text and predefined graphics characters. One is the wide bandwidth of the monitor, which enables it to display 80 characters across the screen with remarkable sharpness. In fact, the dot resolution of the Monochrome Display is far superior to that of the color monitors used with the PC, meaning that individual dots on the Monochrome Display are smaller and more numerous, thus producing sharper images of all characters. The Monochrome Display is capable of displaying 720 dots horizontally by 350 dots vertically. (The Color Display is capable of displaying 640 by 200 dots at best.)

Another significant feature of the Monochrome Display is that the phosphor used on the inside of the CRT is a high-persistence

The resolution of text on the IBM Monochrome Display is
better than that of most other monitors. This is because
each character on the Monochrome Display is made up of more
and smaller dots than characters on other monitors. Even the
excellent IBM Color Display does not display text as readably
as the Monochrome Display.

The resolution of text on the IBM Monochrome Display is
better than that of most other monitors. This is because
each character on the Monochrome Display is made up of more
and smaller dots than characters on other monitors. Even the
excellent IBM Color Display does not display text as readably
as the Monochrome Display.

Figure 5.2 *Photographs of text displayed on the IBM Monochrome Display (top) and the same text displayed on a non-IBM monochrome monitor (bottom).*

phosphor. Once a dot glows, it remains illuminated longer than a typical TV phosphor. Thus an illuminated dot retains a high percentage of its original brightness until the electron beam comes by and illuminates it again. The result is that the display is not subject to what is known as *flicker,* the barely perceived yet eye-fatiguing property resulting from the constant refresh of each frame of the picture every thirtieth of a second.

The lack of flicker reduces the fatigue often associated with CRT use during long sessions at the computer. In rooms having fluorescent lighting, a high-persistence phosphor is almost essential if users want to stay away from the aspirin bottle. Fluorescent lights have a flicker frequency (60 times each second) that is a multiple of the refresh rate of most CRTs. Thus the flicker rate of the light and the video display can interact to provide debilitating eyestrain for the computer user. But because the Monochrome Display uses a high-persistence phosphor and its refresh rate is 50 times each second (instead of 30 as in a TV), it reduces the potential for interference from fluorescent lighting.

The Monochrome Display is frequently said to have a green screen, because the phosphor used on the inside of the CRT produces a green hue when hit by the electron beam. Scientific discussion abounds about the correct color for a monitor. The only thing observers seem to agree on is that the combination of white characters on a black background definitely causes eye fatigue.

Several other combinations are easier on the eyes. Some experts say that black letters on a white background is ideal. Others prefer green on black, black on green, amber on black, or black on amber. The Monochrome Display normally operates with green characters on a black background, but some programs let you invert the colors (to black on green) if you prefer.

Connecting the IBM Monochrome Display to the PC is simple. Two short cables are permanently wired to the monitor. One is the power cable, which has a three-pronged connector that plugs into a designated socket on the back of the System Unit. Because this socket was built into the PC specifically to handle the IBM Monochrome Display, an extra electrical outlet is not required for this monitor. The other cable carries the signal from the display adapter board to the monitor. A 9-pin connector on the cable plugs directly into the 9-pin socket on the back plate of the board.

The Monochrome Display does not have its own power switch. It is controlled by the System Unit's power switch. Whenever you turn on the computer, the monitor goes on automatically. The display's front panel contains two control knobs; the top knob controls the contrast, and the bottom knob controls the brightness. If your work environment always has the same lighting, you probably won't have to touch these controls once they are adjusted for your comfort. But if your environment is subject to the effects of sunlight or other variable lighting, the controls come in handy to make the text readable in practically any lighting condition.

You can choose one of two monochrome display adapter boards for both the PC and the XT. The Monochrome Display Adapter offers only display connection, while the Monochrome Display and Printer Adapter combines display connection with an adapter for one type of printer. (See Chapter 6 for further discussion about printers.) The combination board is generally recommended, because it conserves expansion slots by combining functions.

IBM's Monochrome Display Adapter boards limit the Monochrome Display to text and predefined graphics characters. These adapters cannot produce true graphics, often called *dot-addressable graphics,* in which dots (picture elements, or pixels) on the screen can be illuminated in any combination or pattern desired. Although predefined graphics characters have been used quite effectively in creating interesting images, programs designed to display true graphics will not work with the Monochrome Display.

You cannot attach the Monochrome Display to the IBM Color/Graphics Adapter in an attempt to get true graphics on the Monochrome Display. The signals sent by that board may damage the Monochrome Display. If text and graphics are important to you but color is not, a non-IBM monochrome graphics board that utilizes the IBM Monochrome Display, such as the Hercules Graphics Card, may be the most practical solution. Such boards display the full PC character set (with the same high-quality text resolution you'd expect from the IBM monitor) and true graphics (in one color only, of course).

Makers of PC-compatible computers have learned some lessons from what some consider IBM's mistake: not providing an adapter that displays full graphics on the superb Monochrome Display. Portables such as the Compaq and the Hyperion display high-quality 7-by-9-dot text characters as well as graphics images on their built-in monitors. Many desktop PC compatibles have monitors that display both text and graphics, but the quality of text characters varies considerably from model to model and is not necessarily related to the quality of the graphics. For example, while the Eagle PC's text quality is excellent, the individual dots that make up the characters on the Texas Instruments Professional Computer's monochrome monitor are clearly visible and may contribute to eyestrain.

One caution is in order here, however. Occasionally, you will find color graphics software that will not run on a monochrome monitor. Usually the images from color graphics software are displayed on a monochrome monitor with the original colors converted to varying intensities of the screen color (green on the Monochrome Display). But some programs use color combinations that produce high contrast on a color monitor; in these programs, graphics become almost unrecognizable when converted to similar shades of gray or green. Such programs are usually (but not always) labeled with a notice that a color monitor is required.

The IBM Color/Graphics Adapter
The plug-in board that controls all color and monochrome graphics monitors is the IBM Color/Graphics Adapter. This board comes in two versions: one for the PC and a slimmer model to fit the narrow slots in the XT (see Chapter 8 for a full discussion of plug-in boards). On the back plate of the board are two connectors. One is an RCA-type phono jack (similar to speaker jacks in many stereo components), which supplies composite video output. The other is a 9-pin connector, which supplies RGB video output. The Color/Graphics Adapter has two additional connectors located on the board itself. One is a 4-pin connector to which you would attach an RF modulator to use a standard TV receiver as a display device, and the other connector is for a light pen.

If you plan to use your monitor to display text most of the time, the Color/Graphics Adapter may not be for you, because it

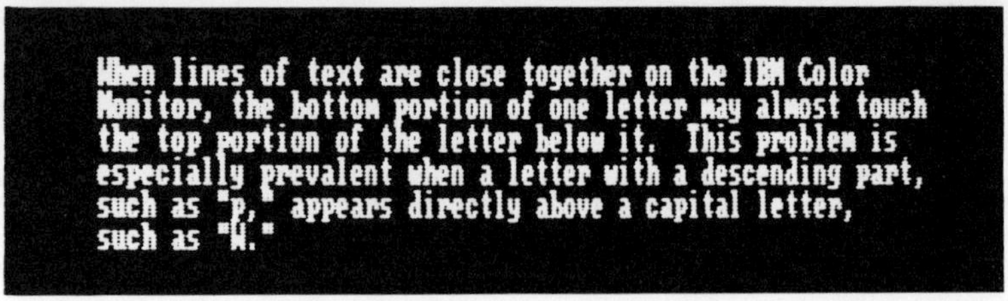

Figure 5.3 *A photograph of text on the IBM Color Display, showing that characters almost touch, particularly when a letter with a descender is directly above an uppercase letter.*

generates lower resolution text characters in the alphanumeric, or nongraphics, mode. Instead of 7-by-9-dot characters in a 9-by-14-dot display on the Monochrome Display, the characters are displayed as 7 dots by 7 dots in an 8-by-8-dot box. Note that these dimensions form a square letter, while the monochrome characters stretch vertically.

The overall resolution of an 80-column text display from the IBM Color/Graphics Adapter is 640 by 200. With the text characters extending so far to the edge of their boxes, you can see that there is little space between the rows of letters (see Figure 5.3). In fact, when a letter has a descender directly above a capital letter in the line below it, the characters seem to blend into each other. For long periods working with text on the screen, this arrangement is not comfortable for the eyes—you will squint, trying to make the letters clearer.

One other feature worth noting when it comes to text display from the Color/Graphics Adapter is that you can't get the same font characteristics on a color monitor that you can with the Monochrome Display. Instead of showing boldfaced or underlined text, for example, a color monitor displays different colors for the affected text.

Color Modes

In true graphics applications, the PC with its Color/Graphics Adapter has three distinct graphics modes. Each mode has a different degree of image resolution and a corresponding number of colors available to the programmer.

The lowest resolution is 160 horizontal by 100 vertical picture elements, or pixels, in a blocklike graphics mode. Each pixel is formed from a 2-by-2-dot box. Although graphics shapes in this mode are coarse, all 16 of the PC's colors can be on the screen at one time.

Medium resolution is used most often for games and other color graphics (nontext) displays. It offers 320 by 200 individually addressable dots (pixels) on the screen. The trade-off for higher resolution is that only four colors can be on the screen at one time, a limitation that is common in personal computers.

High resolution with the Color/Graphics Adapter is 640 by 200 pixels. It limits you to black and white, regardless of the color capabilities of the monitor.

Color and Graphics Monitors

When it comes to displaying color and graphics on the IBM PC, you have several conflicting choices. One option is a monochrome monitor offered by firms other than IBM. Only the IBM Monochrome Display is specifically designed to work with the IBM Monochrome Display Adapter and has the special characteristics described previously. Any other type of monochrome monitor works with the IBM Color/Graphics Adapter and is somewhat like a black-and-white TV.

As its name implies, a monochrome monitor does not display color. This type of monitor generally displays characters in white, green, or amber on a black background. As noted previously, green and amber characters are preferable to white for long sessions at the computer.

Because monochrome monitors exhibit short phosphor retention, much like a standard TV, they are subject to flicker, especially in rooms having fluorescent lighting. But they usually exceed black-and-white TVs in their bandwidth measurement, allowing a relatively crisp display of up to 80 characters horizontally. The text display of a non-IBM monochrome monitor is not as easy on the eyes as that of the IBM Monochrome Display, but a standard monochrome monitor displays graphics well, except for images produced by programs that utilize varying shades of "gray" for contrast. What attracts some PC owners to this type of display is its relatively low cost. Standard monochrome monitors generally cost $100 to $150 less than the IBM Monochrome Display.

Another option is a color monitor. What may confuse newcomers to the world of PC color and graphics is that there are two kinds of color monitors and they differ greatly in price. One is a *composite monitor* and the other an *RGB* monitor, also called a *direct drive* monitor. Putting aside any differences in specifications and quality of components, the prime difference between the two types is the kind of video signal each requires from the computer. One type of signal, called composite video, contains all the picture information in a single stream that feeds more directly into the inner circuitry of the monitor than if it were going to a standard TV. In other words, the video signal goes through fewer conversions than are necessary for displaying a TV image. A composite monitor displays a better image than a TV used as a computer monitor can, because each signal conversion for the TV contributes to a deterioration of the signal finally reaching the screen.

Monitor Type	Bandwidth Rating* (MHz)	Resolution	
		80-Column	40-Column
IBM Monochrome Display	16.27	Superb (text only)	
IBM Color Monitor	14	Excellent	Excellent
Other RGB monitors	14+	Good	Excellent
Composite monitor	12–14	Fair	Fair to good
TV	3.5–4.5	Very poor	Poor to fair

*The higher the rating, the wider the bandwidth.

Figure 5.4 *Bandwidth ratings of commonly used monitors.*

The highest quality video image is produced when the three component colors—red, green, and blue—are sent directly from the computer to the monitor. This is the way an RGB monitor operates; it receives separate signals for red, green, and blue, rather than the combined signal used by a composite monitor. Ideally, an RGB monitor should also accept a fourth signal— intensity—that allows it to display the PC's full range of 16 colors. RGB monitors that do not recognize the intensity signal are capable of displaying only 8 colors.

The bandwidth specifications of composite and RGB color monitors vary from model to model. Those having higher band-width ratings (indicating wider bandwidths) are better suited for tasks that require an 80-character-wide text display and high-resolution color and graphics. If you have a color monitor that has a low bandwidth rating, you may have to view text in a lower resolution, 40-character mode, because the standard 80-column-wide lines of characters are too indistinct for easy viewing. (See Figure 5.4 for more information about bandwidth ratings.)

The least desirable option for use with the PC is a standard TV. Before the signal from the PC can be accepted by the TV, the signal must be modulated—converted so that it appears to the TV to be coming in on a channel. The device that does this conversion is called an RF modulator. You can get one from a computer dealer or an electronics supplier. (The RF modulator that IBM offers for the PCjr cannot be used directly with the PC or the XT because the connectors are incompatible.) When the signal reaches the TV, it is converted again (back into its component parts); these dual conversions result in a deterioration in the quality of the signal—and thus the images.

The bandwidth of TVs is so low that 80-column text display is impossible. Since high resolution is not required for most games and educational programs for the PC, a TV may be acceptable for this small group of applications. But even then, the picture quality will be degraded compared with that of other kinds of monitors.

TV manufacturers have recently introduced component systems. They usually consist of a TV monitor (composite video input) and your choice of tuners, audio amplifiers, speakers, and so on. In general, the quality of monitors in such premium-priced systems provides improved performance for use with a computer. You can use the PC with a component TV monitor and achieve significant improvements over a standard TV, and even achieve the quality of some composite monitors designed only for computer use.

Selecting a Monitor

Probably the first color and graphics monitor you'll encounter is the IBM Color Display. Because it is an RGB monitor that has a relatively high bandwidth rating (14 MHz), it can display 80 text columns across the screen as well as high-resolution graphics. The monitor is priced comparably with other RGB monitors, and it definitely works with the PC.

Not all color monitors work with the PC, however. That is an important point to consider when you are choosing a color monitor. Computer store salespeople are not necessarily versed in color monitors, especially the intricacies of RGB monitor compatibility with the PC. Some dealers even claim that their RGB monitors work with the PC without having tried them. Some of these claims may be accurate; others may be wrong. Many RGB monitors support only 8 of the PC's 16 colors, because signals coming from the Color/Graphics Adapter are interpreted differently.

The surest way to avoid these problems is to buy a monitor from an IBM dealer and insist on a demonstration. A sample BASIC program called Color supplied on the PC-DOS disk displays all 16 of the PC's colors at once (in low-resolution mode). Ask the dealer to run the program, and pay particular attention to the top row of colors, since they are the ones most likely to be missed by incompatible monitors. Make sure that the colors correspond to the color names shown below the color bars. If the colors in both rows are identical, the monitor is not designed to handle the intensity signal produced by the Color/Graphics Adapter and can display only 8 of the PC's 16 colors.

Have the dealer demonstrate some graphics-oriented software on the computer. Programs such as *Pac-Man* (Atarisoft) or any of the dozens of arcade-game translations should give you a good indication of whether the monitor can handle the graphics software you intend to use.

Be sure to test the monitor for text display, too, even if you don't intend to do much text work. Type several lines of the lower-case *m* in the 80-column mode. Look closely at the characters. Are the vertical legs of the letters crisp, with spaces between them? Because of the diffusion caused by the grouping of three color phosphor dots for each picture element, text display on a color monitor won't compare well with that on a monochrome display, but compare two color monitors side by side, if possible. The one with the wider bandwidth and better ability to converge the RGB beams onto their proper spots will probably have crisper letters—an essential characteristic for any text work.

Higher Resolution Monitors

A few independent suppliers are advancing the state of the art of color graphics by offering monitors and special adapter boards that provide much higher full-color resolution than the IBM Color/Graphics Adapter does. These components are used mostly in very specialized applications, such as computer-aided design. Most graphics software designed for general use, however, does not require a special monitor and runs with the Color/Graphics Adapter.

One recent development in using color and graphics is business graphics systems that create high-resolution, colorful bar charts and graphs that can be photographed and converted into slides. Most often, these slide systems are sold as packages that include a plug-in board, special software, a high-resolution monitor, and even a custom 35mm camera holder. Polaroid even offers an instant developing apparatus for its fast-developing 35mm color film. These systems can create presentation-quality graphics at a fraction of the cost of having graphics prepared by outside suppliers.

Criteria for Making the Choice

If your sole use of the PC is for text-related work—primarily word processing, data base management, and spreadsheets—your best alternative is the IBM Monochrome Display and the Monochrome

Display Adapter. The quality of character display in both resolution and readability makes it a superior choice. Don't be unduly influenced by the fact that some of the text-oriented software you plan to use can support a color monitor. The color monitor may look pretty, but the Monochrome Display will be much easier to read for long work sessions.

You should be aware that the IBM Portable PC does not produce the same crisp text on its built-in amber display as the regular PC's Monochrome Display can produce. The Portable PC uses the IBM Color/Graphics Adapter only. The Portable's display, therefore, is the same as what you'd get by attaching an amber monitor to a regular PC's Color/Graphics Adapter. The PC-compatible Compaq, on the other hand, can produce the text quality of the IBM Monochrome Display and the graphics images of the IBM Color Monitor on its built-in green monitor.

If you are set on having color capability, the IBM Color Display or an RGB monitor having comparable bandwidth, focus, and clarity will serve your color needs admirably and still display text adequately.

If text and graphics—but not color graphics—are important to you, the IBM Monochrome Display and a combined-function adapter such as the Hercules Graphics Card (Hercules) are the recommended pair. The Hercules board takes the place of the IBM Monochrome Display Adapter and can translate most graphics output into high-resolution monochrome graphics on the IBM Monochrome Display. For many business applications, this single board-and-monitor combination is more than adequate. Not all software can be used with this or similar non-IBM boards, however. Be sure to verify that such a board will operate properly with the software you plan to use.

If you need both color graphics and high-quality text display, you can buy two monitors. For text the IBM Monochrome Display is the best choice, but you might get by with a less expensive composite monitor instead of an RGB monitor, because you won't need high bandwidth to display text-only applications.

One problem with using two monitors is that the IBM display adapters take up two expansion slots. Some manufacturers, however, offer combination boards that feature both monochrome and color/graphics adapters. Because these boards are thicker than most expansion boards, it is better to use one in the more spacious PC than in the narrow-slotted XT. Before buying a multifunction board, however, try to see a complete demonstration of its capabilities with both the IBM Monochrome Display and the color monitor you plan to use, and verify that it fits in the System Unit if you have an XT.

Tips for Choosing a Monitor

■ Check the bandwidth specifications, and choose a model that has the highest possible bandwidth rating.

■ When considering two or more monitors, spend as much time as possible using each one. Be sure to fill the screen with text or graphics. A full screen provides a much better indication of a monitor's resolution than a few lines of text or a few scattered graphics images.

■ Before purchasing a monitor, use it with each program you intend to run on your system.

■ Have a salesperson set up two or more different monitors next to each other so you can compare their output. For the best comparative evaluation, view a selection of text and images on the monitors simultaneously.

Printers

Although much has been written about the paperless office that the computer would bring, most computer users still rely on "hard copy" printouts of their computer work. For most business applications, a printout is essential for invoicing, reports, and correspondence.

One of the problems with an entirely electronic environment is that most people find reading information on a video screen tiring to the eyes and generally unsatisfying. Editing and proofreading are usually easier on paper. And because hard copy is more tangible, for many people it is easier to work with than even the smallest portable computer holding that same amount of information.

Getting information from a computer onto paper requires a printer. Selecting the right printer for your work will be one of the more difficult choices you will have to make in assembling your PC system. A quick flip through the pages of any computer magazine reveals a bewildering array of printer choices. But because price-performance ratios for printers are improving and new technologies are developing at a regular pace, many excellent choices are available. Let's take a look at the basic types of printers and discuss a subject that few computer store salespeople seem prepared to handle: the compatibility of a printer with the IBM PC.

```
TO:      Alfred Stearns
FROM:    Howard Moore, Jr.
RE:      New bats for baseball league

Because of an unusually large number of broken bats
this season, we find that we are in need of two
dozen more wooden bats; please supply them in our
usual selection of sizes and weights.  We would
appreciate your expediting this order.

In addition, I want to alert you to a change in
status for our league next year.  We will be
expanding from 8 teams to 15 teams.   Consequently,
we will need to double our annual order for both
bats and balls beginning with the 1985 season.

Thanks, as always, for your cooperation. I look
forward to our continued association.
```

Figure 6.1 *An example of text printed by a dot matrix printer.*

Printer Types

Until recently, computer printers suffered from the same problem that monitors still face: no single printer could do everything a printer should do. One type was great for graphics but couldn't produce a legible manuscript. Others did a superb job at replicating the crisp characters of a typewriter but ran too slowly to be practical for "quick and dirty" jobs such as printing a 300-line BASIC program. Moreover, the cost for either high-quality or high-speed printing required a substantial investment, sometimes as much as the cost of the rest of the computer hardware.

Fortunately, with the help of a rapidly growing market for personal computer printers, manufacturers are busy filling gaps in high-performance, high-quality printers offered at affordable prices. Prices tend to fall less quickly for printers than they do for other computer equipment, however, because printers have high mechanical content (compared with a computer's semiconductor content). But with volume manufacturing encouraged by huge consumer demand, prices are slowly heading downward.

The most commonly used computer printers come in three types: dot matrix (monochrome and color), fully formed character

Figure 6.2 *A side view of the printhead of a dot matrix printer. Right: enlarged front view of the print element, showing its 9 pins.*

(commonly and erroneously referred to as letter quality), and typewriter conversions. Each has merit in specific applications. Several other types of printers that are less widely used include thermal printers, ink jet printers, laser printers, and color plotters. Because these printers are rarely the main choices for use with PC systems, they will not be covered here.

Dot Matrix Printers

The first printer you are likely to see in your search is either an IBM Graphics Printer or a similar-looking printer made by Epson. These and dozens like them are called dot matrix printers, because their print comprises a series of dots. These dots form each character within a rectangular grid like that of a character on a monitor. At the intersection of various points on the grid, several dots are printed together in the shape of letters, numbers, and symbols (see Figure 6.1).

A typical dot matrix printhead consists of a single column of 8 or 9 pins, each with a plunger behind it (see Figure 6.2). One of the printer's motors moves the printhead rapidly across the width of a sheet of paper. As the head moves, the plungers thrust pins against an inked ribbon, transferring dots to the paper. In the standard 9-by-9-dot matrix (as on the IBM Graphics Printer), each letter is composed of up to 18 dots. At a speed of 80 characters per second (cps), the printer makes 1440 dot impressions per second. A printer such as the Epson FX-80, which is rated at 160 cps, makes 2880 impressions per second on the paper. (These two printers represent the range of speeds for standard dot matrix printing.) It's difficult to comprehend how anything mechanical can operate with reliability at such speeds, but these printers do.

The legibility of text produced by dot matrix printers varies from model to model and is largely a function of the density of the dots used to form each character on the page. Like a mosaic mural, the smaller and more compactly printed the dots, the more continuous the lines and detailed the image. Some dot matrix printers can even overlap dots to form a continuous line, in which individual dots are distinguishable only with a magnifying glass.

Most dot matrix printers contain built-in software that controls the typeface being printed. Beyond printing the standard dot letters, your computer may be able to instruct the printer to print italic, boldface, compressed, enlarged, or double-strike type (see Figure 6.3). In some instances, you may also be able to further customize the printer's output by using special codes provided in the printer manual. To take advantage of a printer's special features and typefaces, however, the software you use must be able to send the appropriate instructions to the printer. Thus, some programs may prevent you from using various printing enhancements even though the printer is capable of producing them.

Some special combinations of enhanced printing—emphasized and double-strike on the IBM Graphics Printer, for example—can even pass for output from a letter quality printer. Print quality is also affected by the quality of paper you use and the condition of the printer's ribbon. Depending on your needs, you'll have to judge whether the recipients of your work will find dot matrix printing acceptable.

One of the newer technologies finding its way into consumer-priced dot matrix printers is high-density matrix printing. This method can convincingly recreate the fully formed character printer typeface with closely spaced dots, albeit at a slower speed, often without requiring special control codes from the computer.

A few dot matrix printers let you change fonts by pressing buttons on the printer or by plugging in cartridges. One such printer is the Texas Instruments Model 855. When doing standard 9-by-9-dot matrix printing, it is rated at 150 cps. In its letter quality print-

```
TO:      Alfred Stearns
FROM:    Howard Moore, Jr.
RE:      New bats for baseball league

Because of an unusually large number of broken bats this
season, we find that we are in need of two dozen more wooden
bats; please supply them in our usual selection of sizes and
weights.  We would appreciate your expediting this order.
```

```
TO:      Alfred Stearns
FROM:    Howard Moore, Jr.
RE:      New bats for baseball league

Because of an unusually large number of broken bats
this season, we find that we are in need of two
dozen more wooden bats; please supply them in our
usual selection of sizes and weights.  We would
appreciate your expediting this order.
```

Figure 6.3 *Examples of two different typefaces and type sizes printed by a dot matrix printer. This output from the Texas Instruments Model 855 printer is almost indistinguishable from text printed by a formed-character printer.*

ing mode, however, the density of each character is increased to 32 by 18, at a speed of 35 cps. Type fonts are selected by plug-in modules on the front panel. Up to three modules can be plugged in at once, and each font is capable of boldface, shadow, expanded, and compressed type. You can select fonts either through computer software codes or by way of the printer's control panel. You can even change fonts while the printer is running.

Of course, one of the sacrifices of doing special typefaces with a dot matrix printer is speed. A printer rated at 160 cps for normal printing may print at less than half that speed when printing special typefaces. In most instances, however, that speed is still faster than that of a fully formed character printer. In addition to its printing speed, one other reason for choosing a dot matrix printer is its ability to print graphics. If you recall the discussion of video displays, you'll remember that what you see on the screen is a collection of dot images. In printing screen graphics, the computer translates those video dots into printed dots. Not all dot matrix printers are capable of reproducing graphics, however. Choose your printer carefully if you intend to print graphics. Common phrases describing

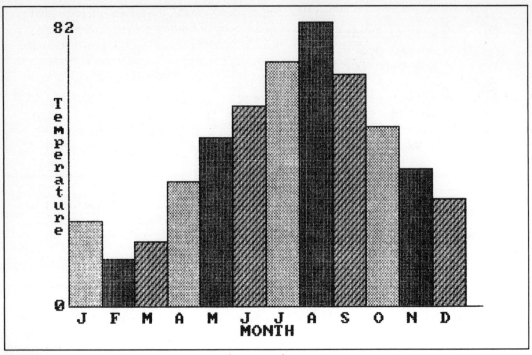

Figure 6.4 *An example of a bar graph printed by a dot matrix printer.*

printers' graphics capabilities are *dot-addressable graphics* and *all-points-addressable graphics*. Both terms mean that the computer can tell the printer to print a single dot in a precise location. Printers lacking this feature respond by printing only the characters in their built-in character sets.

The kinds of graphics you are likely to print in a business environment include bar charts and graphs (see Figure 6.4). Applications programs such as *1-2-3, SuperCalc3,* and other financial planning packages offer this kind of printout if your printer is capable of it. Scientific and advanced math programs also use the graphics capabilities of a printer by printing three-dimensional figures and other shapes.

The IBM/Epson Confusion
When you go into a computer store that sells the IBM PC, you will probably see a printer bearing the IBM label as well as other printers that look similar to it bearing the Epson brand name. Are they the same printers? If not, how do they differ? A little history may help resolve some of this confusion, because many salespeople don't know the differences either.

When IBM began selling the PC, the printer offered with it was a slightly modified version of Epson's popular MX-80. IBM called its version the IBM 80 CPS Printer. Neither printer was capable of printing dot-addressable graphics. Aside from the brand name difference, the IBM version had its own character set built into the printer, which included all letters, numbers, punctuation marks, and a set of block graphics characters.

Shortly thereafter, Epson offered a slightly upgraded version of the MX-80, called the MX-80 F/T, which allowed the user to print on single sheets of paper instead of only the continuous-form tractor-feed paper required on the original version. The IBM 80 CPS Printer did not offer this upgrade.

Epson later upgraded the MX-80 again, this time with dot-addressable graphics capability. This added feature was called Graftrax Plus, but the printer was also known as the MX-80 III. In 1983, IBM finally upgraded its printer, replacing the original 80 CPS Printer with the IBM Graphics Printer. This printer is essentially the MX-80 III with the IBM graphics character set and a few different control codes, which could affect some graphics software output.

Later in 1983, Epson discontinued the MX-80 series (rated at 80 cps) and introduced two new printers. Although the RX-80 bears the closest resemblance to the MX-80, it is rated at 100 cps and has a higher density dot-addressable graphics mode as well as international character sets that can be accessed by special codes. The new graphics mode will probably not be supported by any IBM software until IBM produces a printer that matches the specifications.

An even faster printer is the Epson FX-80, rated at 160 cps— twice as fast as the IBM Graphics Printer. While the FX-80 is capable of dot-addressable graphics, it does not have the same character set built into it as that built into the IBM Graphics Printer. A number of improvements have been incorporated into the FX-80, including easier access to some internal switches (which may have to be adjusted when you use the printer with other computers), the international character set of the RX-80, and proportional spacing.

Another interesting feature of the FX-80 is its "downloadable" character set (if you have the patience and programming know-how, you can create your own characters for the printer to execute). It is feasible that the FX-80 could print the full PC character set, but not without considerable manipulation on your part.

For text-only applications, you will have few, if any, problems using the faster FX-80 printer with the IBM PC or PC compatibles. The differences between the FX-80 (or any other printer, for that matter) and the IBM Graphics Printer are most apparent when you try to print graphics characters or dot-addressable graphics. Because the FX-80 and most other non-IBM printers are not able to print the full PC character set and may not be compatible with some software you plan to use, the IBM Graphics Printer is the most practical choice for use with a PC system. (See the discussion of printer compatibility and printer drivers later in this chapter for additional considerations in matching printers and software.)

Fully Formed Character Printers
Not long ago, this section would have been called "Letter Quality Printers," but with the advances in dot matrix technology, the old lines have blurred. What distinguishes fully formed character printers from dot matrix printers is that fully formed characters are imprinted on the page using the same mechanical principle as a typewriter's. An embossed plastic or metal print element is pushed against the paper through a ribbon, forming the printed character in one strike. For every character there is a separate, embossed print element.

The original print elements in typewriters were individual hammers. Then IBM made the one-piece typing ball famous with the Selectric typewriter series—a marvel of mechanical engineering. What these mechanical typing processes lack in the computer age, however, is the ability to increase the speed at which information is transferred to paper. Two new fully formed character printing technologies have brought speed to computer printers: the *print wheel*, or *daisy wheel*, and the print *thimble* (see Figure 6.5).

The principle behind both is the positioning of an embossed printing element in front of a single hammer that pushes the element a short distance against the ribbon and the paper. As the printhead mechanism moves across the paper, the character elements are positioned in front of the hammer very quickly, offering printing speeds ranging from 10 to 80 cps. A print wheel has each character element at the end of a spoke coming out from a central hub, like petals of a daisy. A print thimble is much like a print wheel except that the spokes are all bent upward at 90 degrees to form a thimble shape about two inches in diameter. Both the daisy wheel and the thimble spin rapidly as the printhead moves from side to side.

With these kinds of printers, you can change the type font only by changing the daisy wheel or the thimble, although a wide variety of typefaces and several type sizes are available (see Figure 6.6). Although some fully formed character printers can perform limited dot-addressable graphics (using the period to print dots), don't rely on them to work with all graphics-oriented software. None prints the PC's graphics character set, although this would be possible if someone devised a print wheel or a thimble that included

Figure 6.5 *A daisy wheel and a thimble (below), the printing elements commonly used in formed-character printers.*

these characters. Presently, a single wheel or a thimble cannot contain enough print elements to accommodate this entire character set.

Although the slowest formed-character printer (10 cps, or about 100 words per minute) is slower than an electronic typewriter with automatic printing, it is still faster than most people type. Generally, the faster the printer, the greater the cost. Slow formed-character printers, rated at 10 to 20 cps, cost approximately $600 to $800, whereas those rated at 40 to 80 cps usually cost more than $2000.

Formed-character printers have been the choice of word processing devotees for a long time. Quite often, professional writers encounter editors or clients who refuse to accept work printed on anything other than a typewriter or a formed-character printer, because dot matrix print can be difficult to read. And lower quality dot matrix printers do not form characters that have true descenders (tails on the lowercase letters *g, j, p, q,* and *y*). They squeeze those letters into the same space given to other letters, creating an uneven appearance and making text even less legible.

```
TO:     Alfred Stearns
FROM:   Howard Moore, Jr.
RE:     New bats for baseball league

Because of an unusually large number of broken bats this
season, we find that we are in need of two dozen more wooden
bats; please supply them in our usual selection of sizes and
weights.  We would appreciate your expediting this order.
```

```
TO:     Alfred Stearns
FROM:   Howard Moore, Jr.
RE:     New bats for baseball league

Because of an unusually large number of broken bats
this season, we find that we are in need of two
dozen more wooden bats; please supply them in our
usual selection of sizes and weights.  We would
appreciate your expediting this order.
```

Figure 6.6 *Examples of two different typefaces and type sizes printed by a formed-character printer.*

IBM does not have a formed-character printer in its product line—at least not with the IBM name on it. At IBM Product Centers, you can buy a thimble printer built by NEC of Japan, the model 3550 Spinwriter, which was designed to be compatible with the PC. The 3550 is essentially "plug compatible" with the IBM Graphics Printer; it attaches to the PC exactly the same way as the IBM printer, using the same cable. It also operates like the IBM Graphics Printer except for the lack of an expanded character set and dot-addressable graphics (the printer is capable of it, but PC software does not support the special codes required to use it).

In selecting a formed-character printer for word processing on your PC, be aware of compatibility considerations (discussed later in this chapter). Try to budget for the fastest compatible printer that you can afford. Professional writers will become impatient with printers rated lower than 30 cps.

Typewriter Conversions
Another option is using an electronic typewriter with a special interface, or converter. Most of these machines use a print wheel mecha-

nism for typewriting. The interface may be a separate box connected to the the typewriter and the computer by cables, or a board installed inside the typewriter case.

The obvious advantage of this type of printer is that you have one machine that acts as both a typewriter for short jobs, such as addressing an envelope or filling in a printed form, and an automatic computer printer for word processing or other tasks. The disadvantages are that the character set is limited to the characters you see on the typewriter keyboard, and graphic representation of any kind is impossible. They are relatively slow (10 to 12 cps is common), and they are more likely to suffer mechanical failures sooner than machines designed to operate as computer printers. It's not that these devices are of poor quality; most are rugged typewriters. But when typewriters are used as printers, the overall number of characters typed is high, and the printing mechanism runs at full speed for long periods, unlike the less demanding start and stop characteristics of conventional typing.

This type of printer is recommended for occasional word processing chores that require formed-character printout, or when there is not enough volume to warrant investing in a dedicated printer. Converted typewriters are best suited for home computers, rather than professional personal computers. It would be unwise to consider a converted typewriter a substitute for either a dot matrix or a formed-character printer for regular use in professional tasks.

Printer Connections: Parallel and Serial

The terms *parallel* and *serial* refer to the manner in which information travels back and forth between the computer and a peripheral device such as a printer. If you look on the back panel of a PC-compatible computer, you may see connectors labeled "parallel" or "serial."

The main difference between the two types of computer communications is the manner in which bits of data are sent through the cable. In a serial connection, one wire transmits data from the computer, and one receives data from the peripheral device. The bits of data, eight of which make up a single character to be printed, are sent one at a time (serially) through the wire. The standard serial connection used with the PC and most compatibles is called an RS-232C connection.

A parallel connection has eight small wires that carry data. When one byte (one character) is sent from the computer to the printer, each of its eight bits is sent through a separate wire in the cable, with each wire dedicated to specific bit numbers (bit 0, bit 1, bit 2, and so on).

The parallel port in the PC and PC-compatible computers conforms to a de facto standard called the Centronics parallel interface, named after one of the pioneer manufacturers of personal computer printers. *Interface* is computer jargon for an adapter or converter. Although Centronics has lost its preeminence in the low-cost printer market, its cabling standard persists.

As you might imagine, the major difference between these two methods of data transmission is the speed of data transfer. At the same data transmission speed, the parallel link sends eight bits in the time a serial link sends only one. But low-cost personal computer printers often operate at speeds too slow to make this difference noticeable—the speed at which data moves from computer to printer through a parallel or serial connection is faster than the printer can print the data.

To compensate for the differences in data transmission speed and printer speed, communications lines in the printer cable enable the printer and the computer to "speak" to each other independently of the data being transmitted for printing. In essence, the two machines have a "conversation," in which the computer asks the printer if it is ready for more, and the printer tells the computer to delay transmission until it prints the batch of characters just received.

Another difference between serial and parallel communications is worth noting. Any time you send an electrical signal through a wire, it generates small, invisible electromagnetic forces around the wire. If you extend the wire over too great a distance, the magnetic force from one wire may affect that of another wire, and information being carried by one or both may become garbled along the way. (This phenomenon is known as crosstalk.) This problem is more severe in parallel printer cables than in serial cables, primarily because serial cables have a greater number of data wires. You will have less interference extending a serial printer cable over a long stretch than doing so with a parallel cable. If you are connecting a printer to the computer, however, you are unlikely to encounter this type of problem.

Connecting Printers

Whether you choose serial or parallel connection will generally not affect your printer's performance, but the choice may make a difference in the way you configure your PC's expansion slots. The permutations of serial and parallel adapters, called *ports*, and their respective peripherals can be diverse.

One of the most common combinations is the PC used with the IBM Monochrome Display and a printer. As noted previously, IBM offers a combination board that includes connections for both the Monochrome Display and a parallel printer, the type most commonly used with the PC. Both the IBM and Epson dot matrix printers have parallel connections. This is an efficient use of a precious expansion slot and makes buying a parallel printer the most logical choice. Unless you anticipate using a parallel-only pen plotter for graphics, there is little likelihood that you will need the parallel port for anything but a printer. (Because most plotters can accept serial or parallel signals from the computer, using a parallel port for your main printer is a safe option, even if you plan to add a plotter to your system.)

Unlike parallel ports, which are used primarily for printers, serial ports can provide a wide variety of services. A serial port is absolutely essential for linking your PC to another computer by modem and telephone line or directly by cable. Other devices that you may not even think about using now, such as speech synthesizers or data-gathering instruments, also require a serial port. It's best not to tie up a serial port with a printer, unless you have extra ones available.

If you use the IBM Color/Graphics Adapter with your PC system, you don't have a parallel printer port on the board. You will have to add a multifunction expansion board that contains the kind of printer port you need, along with a serial port for communications. If you have the Monochrome Display and Parallel Printer Adapter, you will benefit most by choosing an expansion board that has one or two serial ports, since you probably will not need a second parallel port.

When you buy a computer and a printer, you must also buy a cable to link them. Because computers have different physical connectors, even though the wiring and connector pins conform to the Centronics or RS-232C standard, the printer cable is rarely supplied with the printer. Because wiring can vary among cables, it is wise to verify that the cable you buy operates with your specific computer and printer. You may also be surprised at the price of a printer cable: from $40 to $60.

Printer Drivers and Compatibility

Choosing among the IBM Graphics Printer and other brands, such as Epson, Okidata, or any of a dozen or more others, requires research to make sure that the printer you choose is compatible with both the computer and the software you intend to use. Buying a formed-character printer for word processing may take an even more diligent search to ensure compatibility.

At present, except for some simple printer commands, little standardization exists among computer printers. The incompatibility does not involve serial/parallel connections, or how computers and printers communicate, but what the computer is communicating to the printer and what goes on inside the printer as a result.

For letters, numbers, and punctuation, all computers and printers recognize an industry standard called ASCII (American Standard Code for Information Interchange). Whenever a PC sends the ASCII number 65, the printer—any printer—produces the letter *A* on paper. But beyond the ASCII character set and a few control signals for space, carriage return, linefeed, and the like, the printer control codes used are largely chosen by the printer manufacturers. The code for condensed print on one dot matrix printer won't necessarily mean the same thing to another brand. And it probably won't have any meaning to a formed-character printer.

The more features a printer has, the larger its control code vocabulary. For example, control codes are needed for different type fonts, automatic shadow mode (the printhead repeats a character at $\frac{1}{120}$ of an inch or less to the right to produce a solid boldface character), half linefeeds for superscripts and subscripts, and dozens of others. Even the process for underscoring is handled with different codes on different printers.

Now place yourself in the shoes of the programmer who has just written the world's best word processing program. How will that program handle a wide variety of printers having such a diversity of codes? One solution is to insist that purchasers of the program use it with only the IBM Graphics Printer. Such a requirement may be acceptable to people who haven't already invested $2000 in a formed-character printer, but it will turn away many potential customers who have other printers. Another solution is to simplify the program so that it works with virtually any printer. This would mean that only the standard ASCII character set could be supported by the program, omitting any fancy types of printing such as underlining, boldface, or superscript. This solution is also unsatisfactory, because buyers want programs that take full advantage of the features of their printers.

The way most programmers solve this dilemma is to write "printer drivers" for a number of popular printers. A printer driver is initially a separate program that is usually "installed" before you start using the applications program. Typically, a menu appears on the screen listing popular printer models, from which you select your printer. At that point, the program retrieves the special codes for that printer (the printer driver) and writes them into spaces left for them in the main applications program. When you print your document, the program sends the proper codes to your printer.

Printer installation—the process of matching software with a printer—is usually covered in the software manual. When you preview a program, look in the manual for coverage of the types of printers it supports, or ask for a demonstration to verify that your printer will work with it. Make sure that the manual cites your exact printer model. For example, a printer driver for the NEC 3500 series of printers does not necessarily work with the NEC 3550, because the 3550 more closely resembles the IBM printer than NEC's other models in that series. Quite often, the printer drivers delivered on the disk are updated more often than the manual, reflecting the addition of a new printer to the list. You may need to have the salesperson run the printer installation routine so you can see which printers are supported by the current version of the program.

If your printer or desired printer is not listed, you probably still have the option of using a general-purpose printer driver, which is provided with most programs. Unless a software company writes a driver for your printer, you may be stuck with minimal printing features for that program, regardless of the printer's capabilities.

Some programs—the *EasyWriter II System* integrated word processing package (Information Unlimited Software) is a notable example—give you the opportunity to write your own printer driver with the help of questions on the screen. This isn't as simple as it sounds, however; you must be familiar with your printer's commands (usually supplied in the printer's manual) and the terminology of the program. Fortunately, you're not likely to do any harm to your equipment or software by experimenting with printer drivers.

Occasionally, you will run across a printer installation routine that for some reason ignores the IBM Graphics Printer. Instead, the list of compatible printers includes the Epson MX-80 (and sometimes the MX-100, a sister model capable of handling wider paper). In such cases, choose the Epson driver. With any luck, the program will not make use of the features that are different in the Epson and IBM versions of the printer.

Paper Feed Options

You may also have to choose among methods of feeding paper into the printer. Some kind of tractor or sprocket-feed mechanism is standard on practically every dot matrix printer. Tractor feed allows you to use continuous-form paper, which has sprocket holes in perforated strips down the sides. (Paper options are explained in more detail in Chapter 14.) Because the amount of adjustability (in width) of these integrated feed systems varies a good deal from model to model, check these specifications if you plan to use paper or forms having dimensions other than the standard 8½ by 11 inches. (With the sprocket hole strips still attached, the paper measures 9 by 11 inches and is so labeled when you buy it.)

You may need an adjustable width for use with mailing labels, which often have to be purchased in single-label widths because your software may not be able to handle multiple-width label sheets.

On dot matrix printers such as the FX-80, you'll have to buy an optional tractor feed to use such labels.

Many low-priced dot matrix printers cannot feed paper in single sheets (such as standard bond typing paper or envelopes), because there is no platen (the black roller on a typewriter) or friction feed to keep the paper properly aligned. If you intend to print on preprinted stationery and envelopes (instead of mailing labels), make sure that the printer has a friction feed.

Because formed-character printers include a friction feed as standard equipment, you can feed in single sheets. Running continuous-form paper through a friction feed can be tricky, because the paper is likely to move out of alignment after only a few pages. You are better off investing in a tractor feed for the printer. You can buy continuous-form bond paper and use the tractor feed for unattended printing of long documents on a formed-character printer (see Chapter 14). If you anticipate printing superscripts and subscripts, make sure that the tractor feed is bidirectional—that it responds to the printer's platen movements in both directions.

More sophisticated sheet and envelope feeders available for formed-character printers include a sheet guide, which automatically advances a single sheet to the first printing line; a single-sheet feeder, which holds 20 or more sheets of cut paper and catches pages as they are ejected from the printer; a dual-bin sheet feeder, which holds two groups of cut paper (company letterhead and a blank second sheet, for example), feeds the correct sheet when needed, and holds ejected pages; and an envelope feeder, which makes multiple envelope addressing as automatic as printing address labels. Because sheet feeders have such complex mechanics and must be so precise, they cost $1000 or more. They are intended for high-volume office installations where unattended printing is necessary.

Make sure that your software can operate with one of these special sheet feeders. Not all programs send the proper codes to accommodate the automatic advance of a fresh sheet of paper into position or the selection of paper from paper bins.

Printer Planning
The unfortunate tendency for most PC buyers is for their first printer not to really be the right one for the long term. Before buying a printer, ask yourself some serious questions about how you plan to use the computer and the printer.

Most applications other than word processing can be done suitably with a dot matrix printer. But if you plan to add word processing to your system, decide now whether you'll be prepared to buy a second printer (formed character) later—and will have the appropriate connection (parallel or serial) available for it—or whether you should spend more at the outset and buy a printer that can satisfy your future needs now.

A professional whose livelihood depends on word processing should buy the fastest formed-character printer that has the greatest software compatibility. Later, if the need for a faster printer arises, a low-cost dot matrix printer will fill the bill.

Success in buying the proper printer still comes down to one main consideration: plan for the expansion slots and printer connections you will need *before* you choose the hardware.

Modems

As an element of a PC system, the modem is a funny animal. It either figures prominently in the system or scarcely at all, perhaps because a modem is dedicated to one function: computer-to-computer communications via telephone. You either need it or you don't.

The modems discussed here are those used for accessing major data bases such as CompuServe and Dow Jones News/Retrieval, and local services such as electronic bulletin boards. With these modems you can turn your PC into a host computer that provides information to others or a private on-line computer that you can use with a portable computer or a terminal (also equipped with a modem). (There are other, more specialized modems that are not generally used with microcomputers.)

If your telecommunications needs include tying into corporate mainframe computers, the standard modems may be sufficient. But often large corporate computer systems have specific data transfer requirements (protocols) for any kind of terminal or computing device connecting with them. For example, the central computer may recognize only those computers configured to resemble a certain kind of equipment made by Digital Equipment Corporation (DEC) or IBM. In such cases, you would need special communications hardware instead of the modems discussed here. Proper selection of this highly technical hardware is best done with the assistance of a data processing or telecommunications professional.

Modem Operation

The term *modem* is a contraction of the words *modulator-demodulator*. In electronics, anything called a modulator essentially superimposes a variable signal of some kind atop an otherwise steady signal. In an AM broadcast radio transmitter, for example, an unmodulated signal sounds like "dead air"—it lacks audible information. The transmitter's modulator section combines the sound from the announcer's microphone with the steady signal to produce the station's amplitude modulated (AM) signal that you hear.

In computer-telephone communications, the modem works in much the same way. A modem superimposes the computer's internal signals (streams of on-off pulses) on top of an audio signal generated inside the modem. The result is an audible signal that represents the on-off pulses of the computer. To the human ear, the modem signal sounds like two tones alternating irregularly at great speed. In fact, one tone represents an "on" pulse, while the other represents an "off" pulse. When the modem receives a modulated signal, it demodulates it, converting the tones back into straight on-off pulses that the receiving computer can understand. The computer that sends, or initially "originates" contact, and the "receiving" computer both need modems.

During actual communications via modem, four tones (two pairs of two) are used between the two computers. The computer modem that originates the connection sends out information modulated with a pair of lower tones and responds to only a pair of higher tones. On the other end of the connection, it's just the opposite: the computer's modem responds to the low pair while sending information with the high pair.

When two computers link up to telecommunicate, they must first establish which is the "originating" and which is the "answering" computer. The factor that establishes which end is which is a tone sent by the answering modem. This answer tone is the computer equivalent of someone saying "Hello" as the first word spoken upon picking up the receiver of a ringing telephone. As soon as a valid answer tone is heard, the originating modem sends an originating tone. Once the two modems are sending blank carriers (no variable tones conveying information yet), the two computers can begin communicating. There is, of course, much more to modem operation, but such a discussion is beyond the scope of this book.

A modem is only one part of the telecommunications story. It represents only the hardware of a hardware-software team that enables you to put your computer on line. Some modems are supplied with disk telecommunications software that takes advantage of their special features. Other modems need little in the way of software to operate. You may even find software that does considerably more than a simple modem is capable of. Be aware that some advertised software features may not be possible with your modem.

Modem Speeds

If you have looked into computer-to-computer communications before, you may be aware that most telecommunications are conducted at a rate of either 300 or 1200 baud. Baud is a measurement of speed commonly referred to as baud rate. In telecommunications, each character sent over the wire consists of a stream of 11 high or low tones. Seven or 8 of the 11 signals contain the code for the particular character being sent. The rest of the signals are used to identify or check when a stream of signals representing a character starts and when it ends. Each of these signals corresponds to a "bit" of information, just like the bits in 8-bit versus 16-bit computers (see Chapter 1).

Baud rate is a measurement of how many bits are going through the wire in one second. Since each character is communicated with 11 bits, a baud rate of 1 baud (or bit per second) means that completing the transmission of a single character takes 11 seconds. Fortunately, modems operate at much greater speeds. Today, the most popular transmission rate among personal computer users is 300 baud, a little over 27 characters per second. This translates to just under 275 words per minute—a fast but not uncomfortable reading speed.

On the steady rise, however, are 1200 baud communications—almost 1100 words per minute. Communication at this speed is not intended for reading on line, but for fast file transfers between computers. File transfers at 1200 baud require one-fourth the telephone connect time than at 300 baud. Information coming in at 1200 baud should be saved on a disk for recall or later editing, after the connection has terminated.

High-speed modems cost more than low-speed modems, mostly because emerging technology generally costs more than established technology. Because there has been so much interest in 300 baud modems, the current state of the art has reduced most of the electronics to a single integrated circuit chip. The resulting reduction in size, assembly complexity, and power consumption make 300 baud modems available for under $100, a price that was unthinkable only a couple of years ago. In time, 1200 baud modem prices will drop, and modems will probably communicate at both 300 and 1200 baud. But for now, the level of chip integration (the ability to condense many chips into only one or two) is not as high for 1200 baud as it is for 300 baud. The circuit board of a dual-speed modem today contains several expensive chips, keeping the cost of such modems in the $300 to $500 range.

Modem Standards

As mentioned previously, modems generate audio tones to communicate over standard telephone lines. Anyone who has ever talked on the phone knows that there is a considerable difference between the way someone's voice sounds in person and the way it sounds over the phone. The primary reason for this difference is that the telephone line is capable of carrying vocal sounds across a very limited frequency range. It won't pass high or very low frequencies. To make sure that computer communication is conducted with as little error as possible, modem designers keep the audible tones generated by the modem within this narrow band of frequencies. If not for

Figure 7.1 *Three types of modems: acoustic and direct-connect, which are external to the computer, and a plug-in modem, which fits into one of the computer's expansion slots.*

Acoustic modem

Direct-connect modem

standardization, we'd probably have dozens of different frequencies to contend with when trying to connect with another computer over the phone. Over the years, a few significant standards have evolved: not industry standards developed by a particular group, but de facto standards established by popularity, just as the PC has become a de facto standard among personal computers.

At the 300 baud level, the modems compatible with the Bell 103-series modem are by far the most popular. With the 103 modem, the user can switch between answer and originate modes, depending on how the computer is to be used in a given telecommunications exchange.

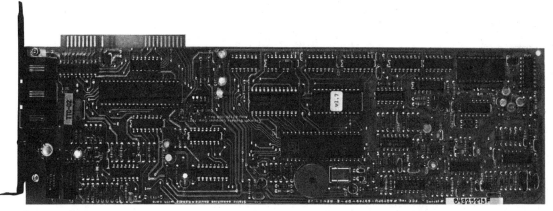

Plug-in modem

The most prevalent dual-speed modem standard today is the Bell 212A style. At 300 baud, it is fully compatible with the Bell 103-style modem. Some dual-speed modems in the answer mode (waiting for your modem to respond to the answer tone) can detect the operating speed of the calling modem and automatically switch to that speed if it is not already set.

Besides these two major standards, there are also many special-purpose modems for specific tasks. For example, some modems are designed to be used as originate-only or answer-only. A possible application for the latter would be using the PC as a remote terminal that only receives calls from a central computer, perhaps unattended in the middle of the night when telephone access charges are lowest.

Other modems offer speeds in excess of 1200 baud. Such modems are expensive, compared with the commonly used modems, and they usually require dedicated data telephone lines—high-quality lines installed by the phone company that cost more than $50 per month just for the privilege of having the line. These dedicated lines assure that phone line interference will not disrupt data communications.

If all the technical differences among modems aren't enough to confuse the newcomer, they also come in three configurations: acoustic, direct-connect, and internal. As you'd expect, each has advantages and disadvantages. (Figure 7.1 shows all three types.)

Acoustic Modems

Many computer users find the acoustic modem adequate for 300 baud communications. Until recently, acoustic modems (sometimes called acoustic couplers) were the least expensive, but that is not necessarily true any longer.

An acoustic modem is easy to recognize. On either its top or its side are two rubber-coated cups that surround the mouthpiece and the earpiece of a standard telephone handset. The cups fit tightly over the edges of the two voice elements to keep the two microphones (one in the telephone and the other in the modem) from picking up any spurious sounds in the same frequency ranges as the modem tones. Sounds like a whistle or the jangling of keys can garble information.

In typical operation, you turn on the computer and the modem. Next, you use a desk telephone to dial the phone number of the computer you wish to access. As soon as you hear the answer tone from the host computer coming through the handset, you push the handset into the cups. Some models have a "carrier" light that comes on, indicating that your modem and the host's modem are ready to communicate.

To disconnect a call with an acoustic modem, you simply remove the handset from the modem cups. When the host computer no longer detects your modem's signal, the answer tone disappears, and the host computer's modem hangs up.

The main disadvantages of acoustic modems are a susceptibility to noise and a lack of useful, sophisticated functions, such as automatic dialing and answering, which are available on other types of modems. And unlike other modem types, they require a standard desk or wall telephone. Some types of telephones aren't shaped to allow a proper fit in the acoustic cups. Even if the lack of features and the need for a telephone nearby don't bother you, the susceptibility to extraneous noise should be a concern if your computer station is in a noisy environment, whether at home or in the office.

A significant advantage of acoustic modems is flexibility. Not only is the acoustic modem usable with more than one computer (should you upgrade or have another computer around the house), but you can also use it while traveling. You cannot use direct-connect modems in most hotels. Because telephones could otherwise be stolen from the rooms, hotels install phones that are "hard-wired" into the wall, so you can't disconnect the wire and connect it to your modem. If you anticipate using your computer from a hotel, you may need an acoustic modem. In that case, however, you will probably be limited to 300 baud.

Stand-Alone Direct-Connect Modems

Made popular among PC users by a model called the Smartmodem (Hayes Microcomputer Products), a direct-connect modem has a jack into which a modular telephone plug can fit, thus bypassing the phone itself. This type of modem is often a compact box that stows underneath a desktop phone, or it can be attached to the side of the PC System Unit (some modem makers supply Velcro fasteners for this purpose). Across the front panel are several status lights that supply a lot of information. For example, one indicator light lets you know whether you are on line with the host computer.

Most direct-connect modems have built-in telephone dialers. Under software control from the computer, the modem can automatically dial the host computer's telephone number. A built-in speaker enables you to hear the dial tone and dialing sounds (tones or rotary pulses) to confirm that the proper operation is taking place.

Another feature worth noting is auto-answer. Not everyone will need this feature, but it can come in handy. Since the direct-connect modem is connected to your telephone line at all times through the modular phone plug, you can have the modem answer the telephone when someone calls and send a modem answer tone. If you have the modem on the same telephone line as your regular phone, you can set the modem to answer after, say, ten rings. By that time, if you're not home, anyone who wanted to speak with you will have hung up. Those who want to communicate with your computer can keep ringing until the computer answers.

This is what computer bulletin boards are all about. Many bulletin boards today use PCs as the system or "host" computer. Messages and programs are stored on a floppy or hard disk and are retrievable by any authorized user. Of course, turning your computer into a host so that others can leave or read messages requires special software.

The latest generation of stand-alone direct-connect modems is of the dual-speed 212A type. Not all brands work successfully with every kind of host computer and modem system you'll be calling. While you will probably not have difficulty with national services such as CompuServe or The Source, host systems for local bulletin boards or specialized services may present some difficulties. Most dial-up services and software seem to work successfully with the

Hayes modem, however. In fact, because the Hayes 1200 stand-alone modem is so popular that it is becoming the de facto standard among PC users, some other manufacturers have designed their modems to be Hayes compatible.

One caution worth noting is that some modems are designed to be used within a network of computers and do not respond to communications attempts with other types of modems. This limitation may be acceptable to you if you are sure that the only communication you will be doing will be among fellow users having the same type of modem. In general, however, try to choose a modem that is as flexible as possible, because you may later decide to extend your communications to other uses. Don't let your modem hold you back.

Compared with acoustic modems, stand-alone direct-connect modems have a number of advantages. Because the connection between the modem and the telephone line is all electronic, data transfers are more reliable. There is no place for extraneous audible noise to get into the data (except in the phone lines). More marginally acceptable telephone connections may be used successfully, since the original signal (on both ends of the connection) reaches the phone wire without having been converted to sound waves. And, of course, direct-connect modems feature both auto-dial and auto-answer, freeing you from having to answer or dial the phone during telecommunications sessions.

Direct-connect modems have few disadvantages. The dual-speed modem commands a relatively high price, but you can buy stripped-down, 300 baud direct-connect modems for less than $100. Although a stand-alone unit may be just another piece of equipment that can clutter up the work area, unused space under the telephone or the side of the System Unit make convenient places to tuck the slim package typically housing such modems.

Direct-Connect Modem Boards

Expansion board direct-connect modems are not new to personal computers; modem boards have been available for the Apple II for some time. Expansion board modems are mounted in an expansion slot of the computer. Dual-speed expansion board modems have many of the same features as their stand-alone, direct-connect cousins. Under software control, the boards can auto-dial numbers stored either on disk with the telecommunications program or in nonvolatile memory (not erased with power-off) on the modem board itself (though not on all models). Most can also perform the auto-answer function.

Since the circuitry needed for a direct-connect modem doesn't fill all the space on a full-length expansion board, some manufacturers are adding other functions to modem boards. One of the most popular combinations is a bank of memory (16K to 32K) and a parallel printer port. The purpose of this combination is to offer a printer buffer for incoming information in case you don't want to save incoming data on disk. Since printers run much slower than incoming 1200 baud data, you could run up some pretty hefty connect time waiting for the printer to catch up with each line of text sent to it. (On some commercial systems, 1200 baud connect rates are two to three times more expensive than 300 baud transfer). But if the incoming characters go immediately into a separate bank of computer memory on its way to the printer, the printer can catch up at its leisure, even after you have disconnected from the host computer.

Having a modem on an expansion board is a mixed blessing: although you have one less piece of equipment on your desktop, you have to forfeit one precious expansion slot for probably a little more than one application.

Internal modems have some other drawbacks as well. One of the most disturbing is the lack of indicator lights. You must rely entirely on your communications software to advise you of improper operating conditions, and not all programs do this. And most board-type modems don't have speakers for monitoring outgoing calls. Most use the PC's built-in speaker and issue tones at rather high volume. Loud noise may be acceptable in a noisy office environment, but not in the home.

Another disadvantage is that the internal modem can be used inside the PC only. You won't be able to hook up your home computer to it—be it a PCjr or an Atari 600XL—whereas a stand-alone modem can be plugged into any computer having a serial port.

Connecting a Modem
In the early days of the PC, if you wanted to attach a modem to the computer, you had to use IBM's Asynchronous Communications Adapter, a short plug-in board. (The term *asynchronous* simply means that the device does not need special timing signals from the computer or the host to transfer data.) The rear plate connector on this adapter was set up as a standard RS-232C serial communications port.

The IBM asynchronous board soon became a waste of space and money. As multifunction boards appeared on the market, they usually featured not only one or two serial ports for communications, but also memory expansion. You are much better off using the serial port of a multifunction board than a single-purpose asynchronous board.

Because internal modems have the equivalent of an asynchronous communications board built into them, you don't have to use the serial port of a multifunction expansion board. But at the same time, if you want to communicate with other serial devices such as a printer, you'll need a serial port on another board—the modem won't provide that capability.

If you decide to assemble your system with a stand-alone modem, pay particular attention to the connecting cable. Because the PC-to-modem connection is unlike most other computer-to-modem connections, be wary of the salesperson who says that he or she knows all about it without ever seeing a PC. The serial connector on boards for the PC has a male RS-232C connector on it. That means that your modem cable needs a female RS-232C connector on the end that goes to the computer. That is not a standard cable arrangement.

Choosing Modem Speed

While 1200 baud may sound intrinsically better than 300 baud, such is not always the case. Since most commercial data base networks charge a premium for 1200 baud service, you must evaluate whether you are getting your money's worth at the higher data transfer speed. On some services, such as CompuServe, the number of times you are interrupted by menu selections cuts into your productivity time, since you must read options and make choices. You may find that 300 baud offers the better value, even if a session does take longer.

If your work involves many file transfers, either from another PC or from a larger host system, 1200 baud will eliminate the time lapses involved in making each transfer. Communications will require less of your own time as well as that of the host system.

The ultimate question, then, is: Which modem speed is right for you? Even if you don't envision needing a 1200 baud modem, over time you will probably discover shortcuts that enable you to take practical advantage of 1200 baud. As long as the 212A-type modem is compatible with 300 baud, 103-type host modems, you'll be covered both now and in the future if you purchase a dual-speed modem from the start. Because most popular 1200 baud modems can also operate at 300 baud, you will have the best of both worlds.

Expandability

Expansion slots are the key to augmenting your PC's capabilities. If you will be telecommunicating information, attaching printers, expanding memory, or adding special circuitry to run scientific equipment with your PC, circuit boards installed in the PC's expansion slots will help do the job. In a way, expansion slots represent your PC's future.

As you plan for the various plug-in options you want to add to your PC, always try to conserve the expansion slots available inside the computer. Although five slots in the PC and eight slots in both the Portable and the XT may seem like a lot, if you buy a PC that has four slots already filled (with boards that provide only essential functions), you may find yourself in trouble in a year or two when you want to add more operations. Because most PC compatibles provide fewer than five slots, expanding them is even more limited and requires careful planning.

When you buy a PC or an XT, you get two cartons of equipment. One contains the keyboard and its coiled cable, and the other holds the central part of your computer—the System Unit—where all the real computing takes place.

Why Expansion Slots?

Today there are dozens of professional and home computers that you can use by simply plugging them into the wall outlet. So why does the PC provide slots and require some of them to be filled before the computer can operate on even a minimal basis? Home stereo equipment provides a good analogy.

A hi-fi shopper can choose either a system consisting of carefully selected components or a compact stereo system, in which radio, turntable, and tape player are packaged into a single unit. If a music lover chooses the prepackaged system, the flaws resulting from compromises made in designing the one-piece system may become more apparent as that listener's appreciation for recorded music increases. Although the listener may want to upgrade to a more capable tape player or a better turntable and cartridge combination, the integrated design may prevent it. The one-piece system may not be able to accommodate new components as they become available, and the system may not be able to adapt to the special technical needs of new technology.

Although a prepackaged computer may have built-in connectors and adapters for a number of accessories, it is still limited to the capabilities foreseen by the machine's designers. Expansion slots in the PC open the way for new applications as technology improves. Since the connections on those slots are pathways to every important part of the system, you can even plug in a board containing a different microprocessor that can supplant the built-in 8088 as the main chip running the show. And because plug-in boards can essentially emulate an entirely different computer, the PC is potentially compatible with other types of computers and software. With an accessory known as a Z80 board (it holds an 8-bit Z80 microprocessor), for example, a PC can run 8-bit software made for the popular CP/M operating system. Another board enables the PC to use most of the software developed for the Apple II computer. Both of these boards let the user add functions of other computers to the PC at a lower cost than buying a Z80 or Apple computer because the boards share the PC's existing power supply, disk drives, and video output circuitry.

Although these two expansion examples show how the PC can emulate less capable 8-bit machines, the PC's expansion slots also allow the computer to advance to applications requiring newer 16-bit microprocessors, such as the Intel 80186 or the Motorola 68000. You can adapt and upgrade the PC to keep up with technological advances while retaining its original powers. Expansion slots offer flexibility and freedom in assembling a computer system that can meet your specialized needs both now and in the future.

Expanding the PC or the XT
If you remove the cover from the System Unit of a standard PC as you are standing in front of it, you will see a power supply in the right rear and a large circuit board taking up more than half the

Figure 8.1 *The interior of an IBM PC.*

area on the left (see Figure 8.1). The power supply takes current from the wall outlet and converts it to the proper voltage and current levels needed to operate the main circuit board, the internal floppy disk drives, or any expansion boards that you add later. IBM calls the main circuit board the System Board, but many computer users call it the *motherboard*. At the left rear of the System Board are the expansion slots, or on-board connectors that accept plug-in circuit boards. The PC has five slots, and the Portable PC and the XT each have eight. (One of the eight slots in the Portable is not usable at present, however.)

Each slot connector is a kind of window to the inner workings of the PC. When a plug-in board (also called a card) is installed in the connector, the board's components essentially tap into as many as 62 electrical and information pathways running through the System Board. The plug-in board appears to the PC as just another part of the System Board. The System Board provides power to run it, passes information through it, and sends instructions from the microprocessor to keep the board in step with the computer's operation.

A plug-in board for the PC or the XT typically has a small metal plate at one end that holds one or more sockets that attach accessories such as video monitors and printers to the computer (see Figure 8.2). This plate fits into the place occupied by a blank plate

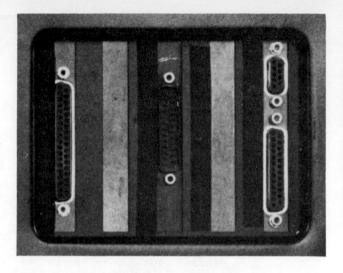

Figure 8.2 *Left: a portion of the back of a PC, showing cutouts for plug-in boards. Right: the metal plate at the end of a plug-in board for the PC, showing connectors for the IBM Monochrome Display and a parallel printer.*

covering each of the cutouts on the rear panel of the System Unit. To insert a board, remove the screw holding the blank plate and remove the plate, plug the board into the socket on the System Board, line up the holes of the board's plate with the System Unit hole, and tighten the screw securely. This simple procedure doesn't require a trained technician; most plug-in boards come with detailed installation instructions.

In addition to the different numbers of expansion slots in the PC (five) and in the Portable and the XT (eight), another important difference is the physical dimensions of boards usable in each. To help make room for three additional slots on the Portable and XT System Boards, the distance between sockets is slightly smaller ($13/16$ inch on the Portable and the XT versus 1 inch on the PC). Thus, the plate cutouts are slightly narrower for Portable and XT boards. When buying plug-in expansion boards, be sure to specify whether you have a PC, a Portable, or an XT. Because two of the slot positions on the XT are just behind the built-in floppy disk drive, these two slots can accommodate only shorter boards. Five of the Portable's slots have room for only short boards. Consider this factor carefully when you are planning for future expansion, because most expansion boards are of the full-length variety.

Even though the XT has eight slots, three are filled at the factory (see Figure 8.3). Two long slots are taken by the adapters for the floppy and hard disk drives, and one short slot contains the Asynchronous Communications Adapter. So the XT actually has only five expansion slots available. Two of the Portable's slots are

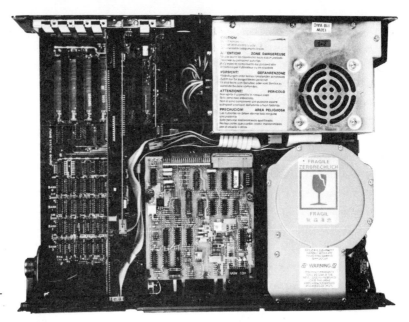

Figure 8.3 *The interior of the XT, showing the three plug-in boards that are supplied with the computer.*

filled—with a disk controller and a Color/Graphics Adapter. The PC, in comparison, contains a floppy disk drive controller and a display adapter, so it has three long slots for expansion.

You're not limited to only the slots in the System Unit, however. IBM and some other suppliers offer an expansion chassis that provides room for more disk drives and plug-in boards. IBM has two models of its Expansion Unit, both of which look just like the System Unit. The only difference between the two models concerns the hard disk drive (see Chapter 4).

Inside the cabinet, the IBM Expansion Unit has its own power supply and eight expansion slots like those in the XT. The two slots reserved for short boards are already filled. One contains the Extender Card, which must be installed in the PC or XT System Unit (thus freeing a short slot in the Expansion Unit but filling one in the PC or XT). A cable connects this board to the second one, called the Receiver Card, which remains in the Expansion Unit. Keep in mind while planning for the Expansion Unit that these cards, or boards, take up two of the available slots in your expanded system.

One last, perhaps critical, note should help you in planning to add boards or the Expansion Unit. You can't place just any adapter boards in the System Unit or the Expansion Unit; some can only be used in the System Unit. These include adapter cards for floppy disk drives, the IBM Monochrome Display, and the Graphics Printer (combination board); a board for a color monitor (when you are using a color monitor only); and add-on memory boards. Most other boards can be placed in either unit. Figure 8.4 summarizes the number of slots available on the PC and XT configurations.

Although at least two slots must be filled in the standard PC to accommodate a floppy disk drive and a monitor of some kind, the XT requires only a monitor adapter board to be fully operational, because it is supplied with the floppy and hard disk controller boards in place.

How Slots Fill Up

Many PC owners are surprised when they realize how quickly the computer's expansion slots fill up. When you bring a PC home from the store, two of the slots are already filled with boards for the monitor and disk drive controller. If you choose the Monochrome Display, the board for it can perform two functions: controlling both the monitor and a parallel printer (such as the IBM Graphics Printer), so that you can add a printer without using another slot. Using a color monitor requires a separate display adapter board, however, and therefore uses separate slots for the display adapter and the printer. To run both a monochrome and a color monitor (one for text and the other for graphics), you need two display adapter boards. Thus the boards for the disk drives, one or two monitors, and a printer could fill three of the PC's five slots. Consequently, your next purchase is likely to be a multifunction board, perhaps one that provides additional memory, combinations of serial and parallel ports, and a built-in clock. Four slots down.

Adding a hard disk uses one more slot, because the disk requires an adapter board. All the slots in the PC are now filled. If you want to add a Z80 or Apple II emulator board, an internal modem, or a specialized local area network communications board, you're out of luck. (If you have an XT with these same boards in it, you will have room for two more boards; five of the computer's eight slots are already filled with the boards you've chosen, and the XT is also supplied with a separate board containing a serial port.)

PC owners generally fill all available slots quickly. Having a few more slots only delays the inevitable. Although you can add the Expansion Unit to either the PC or the XT to obtain more slots, this may be an expensive route.

The problem of expansion slot shortages has not escaped the notice of IBM and other suppliers of PC hardware. Manufacturers are constantly introducing special-purpose boards that combine

Computer	System Board	System Unit from Factory	Minimal System Unit Configuration	System Unit Plus Expansion Unit
PC	5	5	3	11
XT	8	5	4	11

Figure 8.4 *A summary of the expansion slots available in the IBM PC and XT.*

more functions per board to conserve slots. By developing an expansion strategy early in the game, you will be able to upgrade to new features as painlessly as possible.

Buying multifunction boards is the route to success in managing slots. As you map your expansion strategies, think about the functions you will need in the future. You will have to make the most difficult choices during the early planning stages, because you may have to spend a little more for boards that include functions you don't need now. But delaying the purchase of one kind of combination board may only mean that you'll have to buy such a board later and wind up with an extra single-function board taking up space in the computer. Don't let that happen. Plan for future growth.

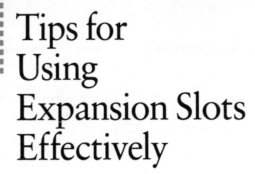

Tips for Using Expansion Slots Effectively

■ When purchasing a memory expansion board, select one that contains or can be expanded to 256K RAM or more. Some 256K boards can accommodate a "piggyback" module that adds another 256K of memory. By choosing an expandable board, you'll be reserving the other expansion slots in your computer for additional functions.

■ Whenever you add a plug-in board to the computer, choose one that combines two or more functions. Multifunction boards commonly contain memory, one or two parallel ports, one or two serial ports, and possibly a game controller.

■ When purchasing a multifunction board, keep in mind that you may want two serial ports in the future. You are likely to need one serial port for a modem and another for any of several peripherals, such as a mouse, a graphics pad, or a speech synthesizer.

■ When planning your use of expansion slots, consider that you may want to add a hard disk to your system later on. Whether the hard disk is installed internally or is in a separate unit, you must add a controller card to the computer to direct its operation.

■ If you consider buying a PC-compatible computer, be sure to check the number and the size of expansion slots provided in that machine. Some software-compatible computers won't take expansion boards designed for the PC. Others—especially portables—have no room for expansion inside their cabinets. Consider these factors carefully when evaluating the price and performance capacity of each computer.

Disk Operating Systems

Computer hardware is essentially useless by itself. This is especially true of PC compatibles that have no built-in computer language or operating system software. What is missing is the element that transforms the hardware into a working computer—software.

Long before you select applications software—by no means a simple task—you must address a number of preliminary software considerations. The most significant decision you will have to make at the early stages is choosing a disk operating system (DOS). You have a few choices, and your decision affects which applications packages you will be able to run, and how adaptable your system will be as future operating system software evolves.

Operating System Software

As noted previously, computers have little, if any, useful built-in software. But there is some software permanently programmed into part of the computer's memory. Residing in a ROM chip on the PC's System Board are instructions that direct other chips and give the computer the unique features that make it an IBM PC.

This software is called the ROM *Basic Input/Output System (BIOS)*. It performs rudimentary tasks, such as scanning the switches connected to the keys of the keyboard to see which one has been pressed at a given instant and then displaying a character on the screen. ROM BIOS instructions in the PC and the XT (there are differences between the two) are copyrighted by IBM and cannot legally be copied by a PC-compatible computer manufacturer. Thus, almost every IBM-standard computer has a unique set of ROM BIOS instructions.

The disk operating system extends the powers of the ROM BIOS to include the disk drives. For example, DOS tells the computer how to control the disk drive heads when they read from and write onto disks. DOS also acts as a kind of converter or translator between your computer's hardware and the software that is stored on a disk. Without a disk operating system, your computer would not know what to do with a program disk inserted into the disk drive.

An important part of the disk operating system is a group of programs—often called *utilities*—on the DOS disk that help perform various disk maintenance chores. With them you can format blank disks to accept data, make copies of disks, check disks for available space, and much more. Other programs are designed to help the knowledgeable programmer get inside a machine-language program to make changes, compose assembly language programs, and perform other complex tasks.

Before you can run an applications program, you have to load the operating system from its disk into the computer. In essence, this readies the computer to accept whatever compatible program disk you next put in the drive. In most instances, DOS software is not included on the disk with each applications program (except the p-System, which is described later in this chapter). The designers of the operating system license its use for a one-time fee, which you pay when you purchase DOS. If the operating system were included on every applications program disk, you'd have to pay the fee each time you bought a program. Instead, you buy the operating system separately, paying the license fee only once, and use DOS with every applications program by loading it into the computer before loading the applications program.

In some form, DOS will be the first program you use at every computing session. If your primary work with the computer involves applications programs, you won't see much of DOS, even though you load it into the computer's memory before loading an applications program. But you will still need to see the DOS utilities for file-management operations, such as copying, combining, and erasing files.

Some DOS versions are more "transparent" than others—the commands you need to memorize are kept to a minimum. The level of transparency is entirely up to the program designers, who tailor DOS to each computer. Unfortunately, as new generations of operating systems evolve, they tend to become more complex and therefore more difficult to master.

The key factor in selecting an operating system for your computer is determining what operating system is required by the applications software that you want to use. At this point, the scales are tipped heavily in favor of PC-DOS and MS-DOS for PCs and compatibles that operate as stand-alone systems.

PC-DOS and MS-DOS

When IBM was seeking a disk operating system to offer with its new Personal Computer, it went to Microsoft in Bellevue, Washington. At that time, Microsoft was in the process of fine tuning an operating system that could be used with the 8086 family of Intel microprocessors (of which the PC's 8088 is a member).

This DOS became known by two names: PC-DOS and MS-DOS. MS-DOS (the "MS" stands for Microsoft) is the software's generic name, while PC-DOS is the specific implementation of MS-DOS for the IBM PC. PC-compatible computers offer MS-DOS as one of their operating systems, usually the primary one. (For a complete discussion of compatibility between the two operating systems, see Chapter 12.)

The first release of PC-DOS, version 1.00, was not the only operating system offered for the PC by IBM. From the beginning, however, it received special treatment from IBM. Essentially all applications software offered by IBM was designed to run with PC-DOS and not with the other two operating systems. Perhaps more important, IBM priced PC-DOS at a fraction of the cost of the other two. The stage was set for the early adoption of PC-DOS by nearly every PC buyer as the primary operating system for the PC.

Independent software developers, most of them not eager to buck a trend set by IBM, continued the swing toward PC-DOS, designing their products to run with that operating system. At the same time, the PC-compatible hardware market was developing. The generic MS-DOS operating system was preferred by designers of these machines, because a large number of the PC-DOS programs could be used with this operating system without alteration.

PC-DOS has gone through several stages of evolution since its release in 1981. Version 1.10 was released in the summer of 1982. Among the new features of this version was the ability to use a serial printer easily with the PC, which had been difficult with DOS 1.00. More significantly for users, the release of DOS 1.10 coincided with the release of IBM's double-sided disk drives, doubling the storage capacity of each drive from 160K to 320K. DOS 1.10 contained instructions that the computer needed to handle the new disk format and assured that the computer would also interpret disks created with DOS 1.00.

The change from version 1.00 to 1.10 was devastating to some independent software developers. Just as version 1.10 was released, dozens of publishers were rushing to get PC versions of their software on the market. Unfortunately, much of the software developed for use with PC-DOS 1.00 was not necessarily compatible with PC-DOS 1.10. Some agonizing months followed as major software publishers who had just released DOS 1.00-compatible software had to convert their programs to operate with DOS 1.10.

PC-DOS version 2.00, released early in 1983, also contained a component for a new disk system—the hard disk offered as standard equipment with the PC XT. The enhancements included in DOS 2.00 for nonprogrammers were primarily targeted at managing the large storage space on the hard disk. A system of subdirectories facilitated grouping related files, and new commands were introduced to back up hard disk files onto floppy disks and restore hard disk files in the unlikely event of hard disk malfunction. Other improvements included increasing floppy disk storage capacity to 360K on a double-sided disk (from 320K).

In January 1984, IBM released PC-DOS version 2.10 with the PCjr computer. Enhancements of 2.10 over 2.00 do not affect PC or XT users; the changes primarily involve the use of cartridges with the PCjr.

The evolution of MS-DOS is not as clearly defined as that of PC-DOS. Each version of MS-DOS, while functionally compatible with a corresponding version of PC-DOS, varies depending on the PC-compatible computer for which it is configured. For example, MS-DOS version 1.25 for the Texas Instruments Professional Computer (functionally equivalent to PC-DOS 1.10) has a number of commands that are different from those on MS-DOS version 1.25 for the Eagle PC. Fortunately, these differences don't often affect software operation. PC compatibles that have internal hard disks require MS-DOS 2.00 or higher.

If you can choose between two versions of DOS for your machine, whether PC-DOS 1.10 and 2.00 or MS-DOS 1.25 and 2.00, always choose the higher revision number, particularly if your work involves sharing or swapping disks from one PC or compatible to another. The advantage of using the most recent version of DOS is that your computer will always be able to read storage disks from previous versions. For example, if someone sends you a data or program disk that was created using DOS 2.00, you can use it. If you have PC-DOS 1.10 or MS-DOS 1.25, however, you may not be able to use a DOS 2.00 disk and could even risk damaging the data on the disk if you try. For this reason alone, you should be prepared to purchase an update of some kind for PC-DOS or MS-DOS at least once a year if the present rate of new releases continues.

CP/M-86 and Concurrent CP/M-86

CP/M-86 is a direct descendant of the popular CP/M operating system for 8-bit personal computers. CP/M-86 is the 16-bit version, designed for the Intel 8086/8088 family of microprocessors.

A newcomer to the PC and the world of operating systems may become confused when approaching CP/M-86, because it is available both from its developer, Digital Research, and from IBM. When IBM first introduced the PC in 1981, the company announced that CP/M-86 would be available for the computer, but the cost was $240, compared with the original $40 price of PC-DOS. Not only was there a big price difference, but the release of CP/M-86 was delayed for several months, leaving computer users and program developers little choice but to use PC-DOS.

In early 1983, in an effort to challenge the supremacy of PC-DOS, Digital Research announced that it would offer a $60 version of CP/M-86 for the IBM PC. Critics of the original CP/M and the original version of CP/M-86 noted that both operating systems were difficult for novices to learn. The command structure was complex and sometimes illogical, and the CP/M and CP/M-86 error messages bordered on incomprehensible. Digital Research's $60 version of CP/M-86 addresses a number of these criticisms by making the operating system easier to use. On-screen menus and function key commands make the selection of operations easier, and built-in help messages provide instructions and explanations.

One enhancement of CP/M-86 over PC-DOS was in being the first operating system that enables the computer to run more than one program at a time. With Concurrent CP/M-86, which is offered as a separate operating system for the PC, you can have a word processing program busily printing out a document while you work with the figures for a spreadsheet or retrieve a document from an electronic mail service. In computer jargon, this feature is called *multitasking*—performing more than one job at a time. Digital Research calls it *concurrency*.

If you were to observe the operations of the microprocessor inside the computer, you'd see that the microprocessor can do only one thing at a time. But because the microprocessor cycles through instructions at a rate of millions per second, it can divide its time among a few different programs. The result is that the computer appears to be running more than one program at a time.

The multitasking DOS from Digital Research, Concurrent CP/M-86, or CCP/M-86, is compatible with most applications programs designed to run with standard CP/M-86. You may, however, find some applications programs that are available in special CCP/M-86 formats to take advantage of a few features built into the concurrent DOS. Moving among applications is as easy as pressing a two-key sequence on the keyboard. Physical limitations, such as changing program disks, are negligible when CCP/M-86 and your programs are stored on a hard disk in a PC having 256K or more of memory.

You may also encounter an operating system in this family that until now has not had many adherents because it requires a special kind of PC setup. It is called MP/M-86 (which stands for Multi-programming/Monitor). This advanced version of CP/M-86 is not only multitasking, but also multi-user. It supports more than one PC, so that multiple work stations can share one machine's software and data files (presumably on a hard disk). Although multi-user PC installations are beyond the scope of this book, when you see this operating system name, you'll at least be aware that it is not some new DOS that your stand-alone PC system should have.

The p-System

One of the computer components that manufacturers and salespeople have forced computer shoppers to consider is the microprocessor used in the computer—8088, Z80, 6502, 68000, and so on—because not every microprocessor can run the same programs. A standard CP/M program, for example, won't run on the 6502 or 8088 microprocessor without an additional plug-in board that literally contains a separate microprocessor (such as the Z80) that is compatible with CP/M.

The basic idea behind the p-System is that a personal computer, regardless of its microprocessor, should be able to use any applications program. The p-System operates as a kind of universal translator; for example, with the p-System, a 6502-based computer (such as the Apple II) appears the same to a program as an 8088-based computer. The p-System derives its name from "p-machine," or universal computer, where *p* stands for "pseudo." It's like putting the same mask on several different microprocessors—a masquerade ball where every computer wears the same costume.

As you might imagine, this level of compatibility among a variety of different computers appeals to software developers. After all, they would need to design an applications program for only one computer—a p-machine—and that program could be run on an 8-bit Apple II or a 16-bit IBM PC without modification. The stores would still have to carry two versions of the program—one on an Apple-formatted disk and another on an IBM-formatted disk—but from a manufacturing standpoint, that is a trivial matter.

The p-System was developed at the University of California at San Diego (UCSD) and is usually packaged with one or more programming languages. IBM markets the p-System with a choice of Pascal or FORTRAN, each in a UCSD version that differs slightly from other implementations of those languages. Each package is an impressive sight, with a total of five IBM software binders. Four are dedicated to the p-System (program disks are included in only one of these binders) and one is dedicated to the language of your choice. The price, however—$695 for the p-System and one language—has surely been a deterrent to the popularity of this DOS.

But you don't have to buy the operating system in order to run software already designed for the p-System. All you need is a low-cost program called p-System Run-Time Support. It contains the barest minimum of the p-System that an applications program needs to operate on the PC. Most p-System applications programs are offered either with or without Run-Time Support. If you are interested in only one p-System program, buy the one with Run-Time Support. If you plan to run several p-System programs and still don't want to pay the high price of the full system (which you would need only if you plan to do programming), you can purchase a separate Run-Time Support package and buy applications without Run-Time Support.

UNIX

An operating system receiving a lot of attention is UNIX, which was developed at AT&T's Bell Labs. UNIX is not necessarily an operating system that PC users will adopt quickly. For one thing, UNIX is intended to help software developers work in a multitasking communications environment. Not all users need that power. And the operating system's commands are rather complex for beginners. In most of its current implementations, UNIX is designed for programmers.

IBM currently offers a UNIX version called PC/IX (Personal Computer Interactive Executive). It sells for $900 and is available directly from IBM, but not from most independent PC dealers. At present very little applications software exists for PC/IX, and this situation should remain unchanged for some time to come. Microsoft produces a version of UNIX for the PC called XENIX. It, too, is supported by very little applications software.

Making the Operating System Choice

Programmers and nontechnical users have entirely different criteria for evaluating operating systems. Unfortunately, novices often read about or receive guidance from experts who have different perspectives on what an operating system should do. It's like having a race car driver cite why a particular sports car is ideal, when what you really need is a station wagon to carry the kids and the groceries. This book assumes that you are not a programmer but are interested in having a PC-standard system for use with one or more applications programs.

The first consideration in choosing an operating system should be the amount of software available for that system. At present, and probably for some time to come, a great deal more software is available for PC-DOS and MS-DOS than for the other operating systems offered for PC-standard computers. Therefore, you should select one of these operating systems (PC-DOS if you buy an IBM computer, MS-DOS if you buy a compatible), unless you have specialized needs for your system that can't be met by software available for PC-DOS or MS-DOS.

There is more to recommending PC-DOS or MS-DOS than the quantity of software available, however. Compared with the command structure of CP/M-86, for example, PC-DOS is less complicated. Neither is simple to use, but PC-DOS is kinder to the novice. You can see more system status information (disk files, sizes, dates, and so forth) with fewer commands in PC-DOS; this operating system is more forgiving when you try to swap data disks in the middle of an operation; and its error messages are easier to understand. And PC-DOS offers a batch file capability, which, once mastered, significantly eases your day-to-day dealings with the operating system. (All these characteristics also apply to MS-DOS.)

Although there is considerably less software available for PC-standard computers that use CP/M-86, some people may prefer that operating system if they have used its predecessor, CP/M, extensively. In an office where CP/M computers are already in use, for example, CP/M-86 may be the logical choice when one or more PC-standard machines are added. Because the workers in that office are accustomed to using CP/M, they will easily adapt to CP/M-86, without having to learn a new set of commands (as they would if changing to PC-DOS or MS-DOS).

Relatively few novice computer users are likely to choose the p-System or UNIX as their primary operating system. If you plan to do extensive programming, however, you may want to select the p-System. If you have used UNIX with large computer systems, you may choose a version of it for a PC-standard computer. The variety of software available for these operating systems may never approach that offered for PC-DOS and MS-DOS, however.

Whatever operating system you use, its developers will almost certainly release new versions of the DOS. In some instances a new release will correct problems in the operating system, but often new features are added to new releases. PC-DOS 2.00, for example, includes routines for operating a hard disk and for creating a series of subdirectories of files; these capabilities were not included in the earlier versions of PC-DOS.

In general, you should purchase the upgrades of your DOS, because software that becomes available for the new DOS version may not operate with earlier versions of that DOS. Most DOS suppliers charge a relatively modest fee for an upgraded version of an operating system if a customer owns a previous version. In rare instances, when a new release corrects problems in a previous version, the supplier may not charge anything, such as IBM's giving PC owners PC-DOS 1.10 if they brought back to the dealer a specific page from the manual for PC-DOS 1.00.

Concurrency and Multitasking

Recent developments in software have made the question of choosing a disk operating system somewhat more complex. Because PC-standard computers can use large amounts of memory (a megabyte or more), they can store more than one program in memory at one time. With appropriate software to direct them, they can also run two or more programs simultaneously. As noted previously, the Concurrent CP/M-86 operating system can direct four programs at once, although the monitor shows the operation of only one program at a time.

Several new programs, including *Microsoft Windows, Visi On* (VisiCorp), and *DesQ* (Quarterdeck), likewise indicate the move toward multitasking for PC-standard computers. These programs are not operating systems in themselves; they are called *operating environments* and are used in conjunction with an operating sytem such as MS-DOS or PC-DOS. Although they do not provide true multitasking, the operating environments allow you to see the output from several programs by dividing the monitor's screen into multiple windows. Only one program can actually be running at a time, but you can change from one program to another with simple commands.

Future versions of operating systems are certain to offer both windowing and multitasking capabilities. Industry speculation is that a new release of MS-DOS will offer true multitasking, perhaps with built-in windowing capability as well.

At present, however, unless you are tied to applications software that runs only on CP/M-86, you will be in the most flexible position from the outset if you buy PC-DOS or MS-DOS and become familiar with it. But if concurrency is important to you now and the programs you want to use run on CP/M-86, you can start out with Concurrent CP/M-86 and related applications programs. You can be almost certain, however, that within a short time you will want to use or try a program that is available only in PC-DOS or MS-DOS, and you'll have to add that operating system to your software collection as well.

CHAPTER TEN

Programming Languages

This chapter provides an introduction to languages for those who are interested in programming on the PC. Designing and writing programs is a challenging task, even for professionals. The first thing you'll need is a working knowledge of a computer language.

An Emotional Choice

You may be surprised at the number of similarities between human and computer languages. Aside from the more common parallels, such as syntax rules and dialects, you also find proponents of each language showing the fervor and pride of a nationalistic campaign. As with operating systems, experts often have one set of goals while trying to guide novices who have different goals for mastering a computer language. A programmer who designs software to control a local area network may not be the appropriate adviser for a part-time programmer who wants to write a program to catalog a stamp collection.

Not only is deciding on a particular language difficult, but several companies each have their own implementations of every language. What makes choices so difficult for newcomers is that there is almost no solid basis on which to choose among a half-dozen C language compilers, much less between Pascal for PC-DOS or the p-System.

This chapter covers each of the major languages you're likely to encounter in your search for a computing tongue. Comments—pros and cons about each language—are directed at people who are making their first foray into computer programming and to those who may have some knowledge of one language (probably BASIC) and are looking for the "ideal" language with which to program the PC. If you are an experienced programmer, you probably already have a good idea of the languages you want to use.

Interpreters, Compilers, and Assemblers

Adding to the confusion about programming languages is an array of terminology that is enough to intimidate the most persistent seeker of knowledge. But understanding the terms *interpreter, compiler,* and *assembler* will help you in selecting a language.

First, let's take a close look at what a language does inside a computer. At the most elemental level is the microprocessor—the chip that runs the whole show. By itself, the microprocessor is not too bright. In fact, the only way it can communicate with the rest of the computer is through an extremely rudimentary language consisting solely of "on" and "off" signals. Streams of on-off pulses pass through circuits, directing the computer to perform relevant tasks, such as turning on the disk drive motor.

Microprocessor designers build into each type of chip a unique vocabulary consisting of commands or instructions corresponding to specific patterns of on-off pulses. It is called *machine language,* where *machine* means the microprocessor and the associated circuits. Computer languages, as we know them, are designed to help programmers formulate a function or an operation in terms that are easier to understand than sequences of on-off pulses.

There are currently two ways to translate computer languages, which humans understand, into machine language, which computers understand. The fundamental difference between the two methods is whether the translation takes place every time the program runs, or just once, after the program is written.

One method of translation interprets the words from a computer language into machine language every time the program is run. An analogy will help explain this process. Suppose a visiting dignitary from Outer Fredonia wants to deliver a speech as he tours our country. Because he doesn't speak English, he must have his speech translated whenever he delivers an address. Unfortunately, the translation process makes speeches take longer; the dignitary has to pause every time the translator delivers a sentence or two in English. This process is similar to using a computer language interpreter. Each time a computer is run, the computer sends every instruction in it through an interpreter on its way to the microprocessor.

The primary advantage of using this kind of an interpreted language is that the programmer can easily make corrections or changes in the program and then test the revised program immediately by running it through the interpreter. The main disadvantage is that because interpreting each program line takes time, an interpreted program runs more slowly than one that does not have to go through that process. And the language interpreter must be loaded into the computer before you can run the program.

If the visiting dignitary had his speech translated only once, before his trip, the translator could read the entire speech at every gathering as if it were being delivered by the dignitary himself. Everyone in the audience would get home sooner. If the dignitary wanted to change the speech for one occasion, however, he would have to write a new speech and have the translator prepare an updated version.

One-time translation is similar to the operation of a computer language compiler. After you write a program in the language of your choice, you use another program, called a compiler, to translate it into machine language. Every time you run the program, you supply the computer with machine language, which does not require translation; it can run faster than if it had to go through an interpreter. The disadvantage is that to make changes in the program, you have to make changes in the original language and then create a new version by compiling the entire program again. Also, compiled programs are generally larger than interpreted ones.

An assembler is nothing more than a specially designed compiler for a particular computer language, which is called *assembly language*. Used predominantly by professional programmers (and dedicated hobbyists), assembly language is about the closest you can get to working directly with the microprocessor short of writing in the 1's and 0's of machine language. An assembler is the translation program that converts assembly language into machine language.

BASIC—Four Ways

For better or worse, one of the first languages most personal computer owners learn is BASIC, an acronym for Beginner's All-Purpose Symbolic Instruction Code. The primary reason for BASIC's popularity is that it is built into many computers, including the IBM PC and XT, although not the PC compatibles. One of the manuals supplied with the PC is a BASIC reference manual. It is not a tutorial, but a detailed listing of all the commands and idiosyncrasies of the three versions of BASIC supplied with the PC.

One version of BASIC is called *Cassette BASIC*. Although you can use all the commands available in Cassette BASIC with a cassette recorder as a mass storage device on the PC, the cassette recorder option is not offered on the XT. Because Cassette BASIC is built into the PC's ROM, you don't have to load anything into the computer to start using the language. In fact, when you turn on the computer without a disk in the disk drive, the computer automatically loads Cassette BASIC into the PC's main memory.

Two other versions of BASIC are supplied on a disk with PC-DOS: *Disk BASIC* and *Advanced BASIC*. Both contain additional commands that enhance the elementary BASIC included in ROM. Disk BASIC has commands that enable you to access disk files, and it gives you control over communications through an RS-232C port (standard on the XT and optional on the PC). Advanced BASIC adds even more commands, focusing largely on what is called *event trapping*—performing a predefined operation when you press a function key while a program is running. It also includes more sophisticated color graphics and a slightly enhanced music function using the PC's speaker.

All three versions of BASIC are interpreted. Although they are easy to test and edit, they tend to run more slowly than compiled programs available for the PC. But for many applications, the speed of interpreted BASIC on the PC is adequate.

IBM and other manufacturers offer BASIC compilers with which you can compile BASIC programs developed and tested with the interpreter. Once compiled, the programs run two to ten times faster, depending on the amount of numeric calculations in your work. The compiler won't necessarily handle every interpreted BASIC program without modification, because it has special requirements for some BASIC commands. These differences are described in the compiler manuals.

All three versions of BASIC and the BASIC compiler available from IBM were written by Microsoft, the company that created PC-DOS. (Microsoft's founders invented the first commercial BASIC language for microcomputers.) The BASICs for the PC are enhanced adaptations of Microsoft's popular MBASIC (the *M* stands for Microsoft). With the exception of a few commands (mostly those concerning graphics and sound), the PC's BASIC is largely compatible with other programs written in MBASIC. Once you become familiar with the PC's BASIC dialect, you should be able to convert MBASIC program listings, such as those from computer magazines or other computers, to the PC.

BASIC: Pros and Cons

BASIC is one of the easiest languages to learn, because the commands are largely derived from common English words. Using interpreted versions of BASIC, you can experiment, change the program, and test changes immediately. Advanced BASIC is among the most versatile BASIC interpreters available for the PC. You can write rather substantial programs in BASIC. *PC-Talk III* (The Headlands Press), a widely used telecommunications program, was originally written in interpreted BASIC. Later versions were compiled for increased operation speed, but even the first version was an impressive display of what BASIC can do.

Few professional programmers would recommend BASIC for commercial applications, however. For writing long programs, such as data base management or accounting programs, BASIC might not be the best friend a programmer can have.

The major objection to BASIC is that it is an unstructured language. You can structure a program in virtually any format you want, provided that you follow some simple conventions such as numbering every program line. Although the flexibility may be desirable for short programs, longer programs require more coherent organization. If a program is not well organized, you can create a tangled monster of commands without realizing it, and trying to trace the operation of the program in search of a "bug" can be frustrating, even though you wrote the program.

One thing to remember before committing to BASIC is that once you become comfortable with the unstructured nature of BASIC programming, you may find it difficult to learn a structured language such as Pascal.

Pascal

There are many advocates of the Pascal language. As a compiled language, it runs rings around BASIC in performance. One of the most popular word processing programs for the PC, *Volkswriter* (Lifetree Software), was written in Pascal and demonstrates impressive speed. Pascal is a favorite language in high school and college computer programming classes, and some people assert that because Pascal is a structured language, you will find other languages easier to learn if Pascal is the first computer language you learn. It is one of the few programming languages named after an individual—pioneer mathematician Blaise Pascal—rather than as an acronym for a technical phrase.

Unfortunately, various versions of Pascal do not share a common syntax such as that seen among versions of MBASIC. Some standards were established for Pascal, but in efforts to be unique in the marketplace, different Pascal suppliers have made enhancements to the language that preclude a high degree of compatibility from one Pascal version to another.

For the PC, you can choose among several versions of Pascal, for both PC-DOS and CP/M-86. IBM also offers a version of Pascal (UCSD Pascal) for the p-System. The execution speed of programs written in UCSD Pascal is not as great as that of versions written for the other operating systems, however.

COBOL

One of the most venerable languages in the world of business computing is COBOL, an acronym for Common Business-Oriented Language. Developed in the early 1960s, COBOL has been a popular language among mainframe and minicomputer programmers. A COBOL program can be changed relatively easily, because its commands conform to a rigid structure and have fewer variations than those of other languages.

COBOL applications on the PC are generally restricted to the business environment. Programs originally written in COBOL for other computers can be put through the PC's COBOL compiler and run on the PC. A business programmer can write a COBOL program on the PC, then use it on the company's expensive minicomputer.

FORTH

FORTH was first used in 1969 to help astronomers control giant telescopes with computers. Since then, it has become one of the fastest operating, most compact languages (in terms of memory used up by the finished, compiled program) available for microcomputers.

Like Pascal, FORTH is a structured language, but it offers the programmer more leeway to improvise while writing than Pascal does. IBM does not market a version of FORTH, but several independent suppliers offer versions for the PC.

FORTRAN

Another old-timer in the world of computer languages is FORTRAN (short for Formula Translation), which was originally developed for scientific applications. Its forte is handling numbers and complex mathematics. FORTRAN is still taught in the computer science departments of many colleges, but it is almost exclusively used for math and science applications. FORTRAN compilers for the PC are available from both IBM and Microsoft.

C

Not to be confused with Digital Research's CBASIC, the C language is perhaps one of the fastest growing in popularity among professional programmers. A surprising number of applications and entertainment software for the PC are written in C. It may be a significant language in the future, because it is closely associated with the UNIX operating system, which could possibly become the primary operating system of the next generation of 32-bit personal computers.

Several suppliers offer versions of C for the PC. The Digital Research versions of C (one for CP/M-86 and another for MS-DOS) come with the text from the "bible" of C programmers, *C Programming Language* (Prentice-Hall, 1978), written by the language's developers, Brian W. Kernighan and Dennis M. Ritchie.

The highly regarded benefits of the C language are compact programs and fast execution. But for occasional, short programming, you will probably be better off learning Pascal or BASIC.

Logo

Programming in Logo is fun. This graphics-oriented language attracts the attention of people who are not ordinarily interested in programming. Logo was originally designed at MIT as an educational aid to help students learn both computers and geometry. Its commands are largely in English, and the results of commands can be viewed on the screen almost immediately. Although the language can be used for some business-oriented applications, its strength is as a computer learning tool. Because Logo is a structured language, using it instills good programming habits that can carry over to more sophisticated languages such as Pascal and C.

Choosing a Language

Although other programming languages are available for the PC, you'll hear most about those already mentioned. If you plan to do programming for yourself, with no intention of getting into the commercial software business, Advanced BASIC (and perhaps the BASIC Compiler) will probably be more than adequate. Do investigate Pascal, however, because you may want to extend your programming skills beyond the limitations of BASIC. If you think you'll want to do commercial programming, consider the structured languages such as Pascal, FORTH, and C.

If you're new to programming, be prepared to spend a great deal of time learning the language you choose. Just like a spoken language, the more you use it and learn from your mistakes, the sooner you begin to feel comfortable with it. No matter how much you learn about a language, you will always find someone who knows more about it than you do. Take advantage of the opportunity to learn from fellow programmers.

Applications Programs

The first step in making a successful personal computer purchase is mapping out precise uses for the machine. Consider what you will be doing with the computer not only the week you bring it home but also the following year. This is particularly critical if you buy an IBM PC, because the way you configure your system will affect the ease with which you can expand your system and its operations in the future.

As often happens, someone is introduced to computers by a friend or a business colleague. Amazed by the computational wonders demonstrated in a limited application, the newly enlightened consumer rushes out to buy a computer that functions the same way. But as that new user becomes more comfortable with the computer and does further reading about it, he or she discovers that the computer can do a lot more than the limited applications originally witnessed.

With the IBM PC and some compatibles, that discovery could be a costly one. To meet the immediate application goals, the user probably chose add-on boards, disk drives, and a monitor that did not necessarily satisfy the requirements of applications discovered later. There may be no room for a needed add-on board. Or a costly new monitor may be required to replace one that cannot accommodate the new applications.

This chapter examines the major types of applications and the ways you can use them, the system requirements for these applications, the way some applications evolve into others, and how you should be prepared for growth in these areas.

Personal computer applications programs are generally of five basic types: financial management (including spreadsheets), word processing, data base management, telecommunications, and graphics. Unfortunately, someone interested in spreadsheets may overlook most of the other categories without fully understanding how they can be used. An executive who is a spreadsheet expert may believe that word processing is only for writers or secretaries, or that graphics software is only for artists. Yet that very executive may be more effective on the job if he or she could combine the powers of all three applications to create forecasts, budgets, proposals, and reports.

Today, distinctions among these five categories are blurring, thanks to a new generation of software called *integrated software*. Integrated programs combine several applications. Because these programs usually share a common base of stored information, you don't have to retype or copy information when going, for example, from data base management to word processing.

Financial Management
The financial management category of applications software includes a rather diverse collection of programs, some of which may be used daily in a business, while others are used occasionally for specific jobs such as monthly forecasting. Each one places different demands on the computer system.

The regular tasks include accounting, payroll, and inventory. This work applies to professionals and to manufacturing and service companies. A physician or an attorney, even one who has outside accounting help, may find a billing (receivables) program useful in tracking monies due. A small office, however, may not need an expensive software system for payables, since they represent a relatively small percentage of the firm's monthly financial transactions.

Accounting software ranges from individual programs for payables, receivables, and general ledger to completely integrated programs (or a linked series of programs), which minimize the amount of repetition required while entering information. An all-in-one accounting program is generally simpler to use, but it may not accommodate all of your accounting needs. In an integrated program or a linked series of modules, you use each module for its appropriate task, and the data is automatically shared with other modules. For example, payables programs can track a company's outgoing funds, distribute amounts into account categories, and print checks. Receivables software can generate invoices and a variety of reports, including aging data (that is, amounts customers have not paid, and how much money is overdue by 30, 90, or 120 days, for example). The information entered for both payables and receivables is then automatically posted to the general ledger component.

The complexity of an accounting program and its computer system requirements depend to a large extent on the anticipated number of transactions. These programs are usually divided into modules, each of which requires no more than 64K of memory. And while the program publisher's advertising may suggest that you can get by with one disk drive, two drives are recommended for accounting. You will be storing financial data on a separate disk from the program disk. And because the computer needs to reach into the program disk for other modules (going from payables to receivables, for example), you'll avoid a lot of disk swapping by running the program with the program disk in one drive and the data disk in the other. Because some programs have you swapping two or more program disks in one drive to get from one module to another, anything you can do to reduce disk swapping will be simpler in the long run. And program manuals generally favor the two-disk-drive method.

Since you will be maintaining vital information on the data disks, you should not only prepare to make backup copies after every session, but also develop a system that allows you to store one copy off the premises. At the same time, find a place in the office—a safe or a vault, perhaps—where the primary copies are secure from theft or fire. These precautions are no more complex than those taken for the same records on paper.

Double-sided disk drives (360K capacity) are the rule in accounting. Because you will want to store as much information as possible on a single disk, the larger capacity disk drives are preferable for convenience and ease of organization of archived material. In fact, the higher density disk drives, such as the 720K drives on the Tandy 2000, make some of the PC-compatible computers attractive, provided that the software you need is available on that computer. Large-capacity disk storage can be a valuable, time-saving tool if your business involves several hundred transactions every month. Because many accounting packages do not let you carry over a monthly accounting period from one disk to another, one blank disk must be capacious enough to store an entire month's records.

The number of transactions recordable on a disk varies with each software package, but if you plan for surplus space on your data disks, you will be able to accommodate growth for some time to come.

If accounting programs are one of the primary uses of a computer in your business and an operator devotes a lot of time each day to that task, a hard disk may be appropriate for your system. A hard disk, usually having at least the capacity of about 30 double-sided disks, accommodates more transactions within a given accounting period. Another benefit of a hard disk system is that an accounting program comprising several modules (and designed for transfer to a hard disk) can be permanently maintained on the hard disk. You won't have to swap program disks to get from payables to receivables, for example, and the changeover time will be significantly less.

Because expensive accounting packages are likely to be copy protected, you cannot transfer them from the floppy disks on which the program is supplied to a hard disk. Of course, with the proliferation of XTs and similar hard-disk-based PC compatibles, software publishers are making provisions for a single copy to be made to a hard disk. This is one factor to investigate carefully when you select software.

Archival storage of information on a hard disk is not maintenance-free or limitless. If you run several applications on your PC (such as word processing and inventory programs in addition to accounting), you will want room on the hard disk for both the programs and the data files for each program. Any experienced PC owner can tell you that it doesn't take long to fill up 30 double-sided disks with programs and data. Don't expect a hard disk to be a permanent archival storage area for accounting data.

If you use a hard disk system for accounting, the operator in charge of that application should have a daily procedure for backing up all new data on floppy disks (or another backup medium). The same precautions about storing floppy disks overnight should be taken with the backup media. If you back up all your data and keep disks in a safe place, you can easily reload all the information into a replacement machine without delay in the event of theft or damage to the computer.

Electronic spreadsheets are among the most popular programs for personal computers. They essentially recreate a ledger sheet on the computer screen (see Figure 11.1). Just as you might do with paper and pencil, you can label rows and columns with headings and enter any kind of numbers you need for your forecast or other number management tasks. The electronic version surpasses its paper and pencil ancestor in its use of boxes, or *cells*. For example, you might dedicate the cells to subtotals and totals, and then use formulas to perform calculations such as adding up the appropriate columns and rows. As you change numbers in some cells, the totals are automatically recalculated to reflect your changes. The formulas can

```
A20  (L)  NET                                                    C
                                                                 279
        A       B       C       D       E       F       G       H
  4 Salary    15000   17500   21000   26000
  5 Consult    1700    3270    7835    9200
  6 Photos      700     620    1026     940
  7 Art        1055     588     680     760
  8 Subtotal  18455   21978   30541   36900
  9
 10 EXPENSES
 11 Assistant     0       0    3600    6000
 12 Film        144     187     241     226
 13 Paints       76     104      90     137
 14 Brochure      0       0     481     159
 15 Paper        44      82      63     119
 16 Phone        84      66     107     145
 17 Bus. card     0      46       0      71
 18 Subtotal    348     485    4582    6857
 19
 20 NET       18107   21493   25959   30043
 21
 22
 23
 24
```

Figure 11.1 *A photograph of the IBM Monochrome Display showing a* VisiCalc *worksheet.*

be rather complex, if necessary, including built-in functions such as averages, net present value, logs, and even trigonometric functions.

Electronic spreadsheets enable you to create massive worksheets inside the computer, even though your screen may display only 6 columns across and 20 rows down at one time. The screen acts as a window on whatever size spreadsheet you create. Some programs can handle spreadsheets that would fill an office wall if they were done on paper.

One significant benefit of electronic spreadsheets is that they enable managers to experiment with numbers for forecasts, sales results, and budgets without having to do repetitive math with a calculator. If the figures don't look just right, you can go back and try a new number here and there to make the totals come out right.

VisiCalc (VisiCorp) was the program that launched the electronic spreadsheet concept. You can still buy *VisiCalc* for the PC, but other, more powerful programs have come along to challenge *VisiCalc*'s popularity. *Multiplan* (Microsoft) is preferred by many spreadsheet users, and *SuperCalc* (Sorcim) also has a group of enthusiastic users.

Some enhanced spreadsheet programs combine limited data base management and business graphics capabilities. True integrated software can even combine complete programs, such as word processing and other applications software. Broad-based integrated software is covered later in this chapter. For now, let's focus on integrated software whose basic strength is the electronic spreadsheet.

The most popular program of this kind is *1-2-3* (Lotus Development). More recently, *SuperCalc3* (Sorcim) has joined the ranks of high-quality integrated spreadsheet software. Both of these programs use an electronic spreadsheet as the background for sophisticated spreadsheet calculations (having more built-in math functions, for example, than spreadsheet-only programs). Within the spreadsheet, you can enter lists of names into cells, and have the program sort them according to criteria that you specify, thus performing data base operations.

These programs can also take information directly from the spreadsheet and convert it into graphics such as bar graphs, line graphs, and pie charts. You don't have to reenter the data to get the graphics. And as you alter the data in the spreadsheet, both the totals and the graphics representations change accordingly.

Because integrated spreadsheets such as *1-2-3* place special hardware requirements on the PC, buying this type of program requires more forethought than others. Most of these programs require a minimum of 128K of RAM (*1-2-3*, in fact, requires 192K). They treat RAM *dynamically*—the more memory you have installed in the computer, the more the program can use to keep a big spreadsheet in active memory. You might easily find your spreadsheet size limited if you have only the recommended 128K of memory. Because these programs are themselves rather large and take up a good portion of memory, it's best to have at least 256K of RAM.

Another aspect of planning involves graphics. Some users may see graphics as an unnecessary frill, but experienced users will tell you that graphics can really enhance a presentation. Displaying graphics requires the IBM Color/Graphics Adapter for the PC or the XT, or a similar capability in a PC compatible. If you prefer the IBM Monochrome Display for your text work, you will need a color monitor and adapter board just for graphics, or a special monochrome graphics board, such as the Hercules Graphics Card, which displays monochrome graphics on the IBM Monochrome Display.

Even if you have two monitors, you can't have two active screens at one time—you can work with only one monitor at a time. If you want to see a pie chart of your spreadsheet data, the spreadsheet on the Monochrome Display freezes while the color monitor is being used. When control is returned to the Monochrome Display, the graphics image is frozen on the color monitor. As you make changes in your numbers, the results won't show up on the color monitor until you switch control over to it again. Unless color is important to you, the Hercules-type board and monochrome monitor combination is probably a practical solution. (Be sure that a specialized adapter board will work with all your software, however.)

If most of your other computer work involves color graphics, you can perform all your integrated spreadsheet work on a color monitor, even though the rows and the columns of numbers won't be as easy on the eyes as they are with the Monochrome Display.

Most PC compatibles have the ability to display graphics on their monochrome screens. The Compaq portables are such an example. You get the full graphics features of the software, except the color. If necessary, a color monitor can usually be connected to the computer for color graphics.

Printers are another consideration for use with all types of financial management software. Unless you must use an electronic spreadsheet program to create a fancy presentation or a payables program to print checks, you can usually get by quite well with a dot matrix printer. Matrix printers that let you print in both draft and letter quality modes, plus graphics, will handle every financial management printing task.

One printer feature to consider for financial work is carriage width. You can choose a standard-width (80-column) or extra-width (132-column) printer. Because the reports produced using accounting or spreadsheet programs often exceed 80 columns, a 132-column printer is recommended for this application. You can also use an 80-column dot matrix printer that offers a condensed font. Although it can print 132 columns of characters on 8½-inch-wide paper, the characters will be smaller and very close together.

Be sure to try your software on various printers before you buy one, to make sure that the printer is supported by the software, that the printer can accommodate the report sizes you require, and that the printer will also work well with the other programs and applications that you intend to use.

Word Processing

Although computers were originally designed to manipulate numbers, many PCs and compatibles are being purchased to manipulate words. Word processing software turns the PC and the printer into a facile electronic typewriter with the memory of an elephant. Word processing is one of the most productive applications on the PC. Any time a memo, a report, an article, or a book needs to be retyped, a word processing PC starts paying for itself by eliminating the need to retype sections that don't need fixing. All you have to do is type in the corrections (including moving paragraphs around and deleting passages), save the work, and give the print command. While the printer spews out your revised document at 200 to 400 words per minute, you can do something else. (Figure 11.2 shows the primary operations of a major word processing program.)

Because even the simplest word processing tasks are such a vast improvement over the typewriter, word processing novices tend to start out with the bare minimum of memory and disk drive capacity specified by the software publisher. Although the system may at first seem adequate, they will probably want to learn other techniques later to increase productivity, and may then need more than the minimum configuration. As always, try to think ahead.

Most word processing programs are designed to work on a 64K or 128K RAM system, even if they can take advantage of more memory. If the program uses up a lot of RAM, however, you may have enough room in memory for only a handful of pages at any one time.

Word processing is often divided into linked program modules. The pieces of the puzzle remain invisible to you because you don't have to load in the pieces as they are needed. The program does the loading automatically, as in *WordStar* (MicroPro), currently the most popular word processing program. At first, you probably won't pay much attention when the program reaches out to the program disk for instructions; you'll be thankful that your keystrokes are being recorded. As you become familiar with the program, you will be picking up speed, and will soon find yourself waiting for the computer to get its next instructions—you'll be twiddling your thumbs while the program figures out what it needs to do next. This is frustrating to an experienced user—which you will soon become.

The way around this delay is to equip your PC with at least 256K of RAM and a disk emulation program, which treats part of memory as an electronic disk drive. Provided that your word processing program is not copy protected (*WordStar,* for example, is not), you can copy all the program files from the floppy disk to the electronic disk each time you start up the program, and thereby avoid having to wait for the program to retrieve a module from the floppy disk.

Keeping a document, with all its revisions, in an electronic disk during a word processing session can be dangerous: if the power goes out or the computer or the program malfunctions, your work will be wiped out. Be sure to save your work to a floppy disk approximately every 15 minutes.

Disk drive configuration is a matter of debate among word processing users. Those who have hard disks wouldn't trade them for floppies at any price, but many professional writers manage quite

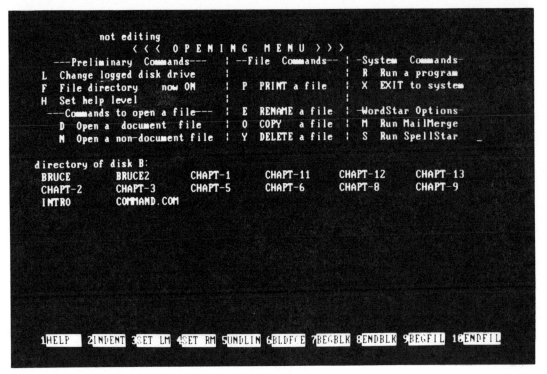

```
          not editing
                  < < < O P E N I N G   M E N U > > >
       ---Preliminary  Commands---    : --File  Commands-- : -System  Commands-
    L  Change logged disk drive       :                    : R  Run a program
    F  File directory      now ON     : P  PRINT a file     : X  EXIT to system
    H  Set help level                 :                     :
       ---Commands to open a file---   : E  RENAME a file   : -WordStar Options-
       D  Open a  document  file       : O  COPY   a file   : M  Run MailMerge
       N  Open a non-document file     : Y  DELETE a file   : S  Run SpellStar

  directory of disk B:
    BRUCE        BRUCE2       CHAPT-1      CHAPT-11     CHAPT-12    CHAPT-13
    CHAPT-2      CHAPT-3      CHAPT-5      CHAPT-6      CHAPT-8     CHAPT-9
    INTRO        COMMAND.COM




    1HELP    2INDENT 3SET LM 4SET RM 5UNDLIN 6BLDFCE 7BEGBLK 8ENDBLK 9BEGFIL 10ENDFIL
```

Figure 11.2 *A photograph of the IBM Monochrome Display showing the* WordStar *opening menu.*

well with two floppy disk drives. Nonetheless, some word processing tasks make a hard disk a welcome part of the system.

A 360K double-sided disk drive can hold approximately 180 double-spaced pages of documents. When the disk is full, you have to store it away and prepare a new one. Disks fill up twice as fast with some programs, because they automatically create a backup copy of each file. If your work is such that you don't have to refer frequently to previous work once it is completed, floppy disk storage is adequate. Retrieving a document that you wrote a couple of months ago presents no problems if you do it occasionally, as long as you have a handy directory of the contents of each data disk in your archives.

The limit to disk capacity should not affect your work, however. Word processing software generally limits the size of any single document in memory to about 40 pages, but programs generally begin to operate a bit sluggishly as soon as the document exceeds 20 pages or so. Thus, you will want to divide long chapters into smaller sections, regardless of disk capacity.

If you put the word processing program on an electronic disk, you have two floppy disk drives (if you follow our recommendation to buy a PC with no fewer than two drives) and access to about 360 pages of work without having to swap disks. This can be useful for such tasks as printing a series of files.

Certain types of word processing tasks benefit from the greater storage capacity of a hard disk. Work involving form letters or linking standard forms, such as contracts, will best be served by storing those frequently used text modules on the hard disk (along with the program). You would still use a floppy disk for storing the current document.

A hard disk is particularly useful for working with several book-length documents at once. It's not that floppies can't handle the documents, but having the documents all on a hard disk means fewer floppies to keep track of and more convenient ways to locate a precise section of text needed at any given moment. You will still need floppies for backup copies, of course, after every session involving revisions to the text.

As far as monitors for word processing go, nothing can top the high resolution of the IBM Monochrome Display or the monitor built into the IBM and Compaq portable computers. Long sessions in front of a color monitor, with its slightly fuzzy, lower resolution characters, are tough on the eyes.

Serious word processing users will want the professional appearance of documents printed on a letter quality printer, either of the formed-character or high-resolution dot matrix type. (See Chapter 6 for a detailed discussion of printers.)

Many professional writers are required to send finished documents to an editor or a typesetter via modem. (This process is discussed at length in the section on telecommunications later in this chapter.) Even if your assignments today don't call for telephone transmission of documents, they may in the future, so if you are a professional writer, prepare your PC for the addition of a modem.

Data Base Management

A hard disk is especially well suited to using a data base management program, which is a sophisticated electronic filing system. Data base software lets you design a form—an index card, a patient record, a customer file, a personnel record, or any of hundreds of possibilities—on which you enter information in response to the questions on the screen. This information is stored on disk until you need to retrieve all or part of it. A data base manager lets you search and sort the records according to any criteria you establish (such as everyone born between 1940 and 1948). While a filing cabinet can store information in only one way—usually alphabetically—the computer can search through the contents of every record and arrange your files in any way you specify, such as by zip code, city, account balance, and so forth. Many data base programs have a report component that lets you design a printout of the information you're requesting.

A data base management program is one of the more powerful programs you're likely to run on the PC. It relies, obviously, on a large base of data—the information you type in. If that data must be handy at all times because you must access the files at a moment's notice, having the data base and its search program on a hard disk will give you the feeling of having that information at your fingertips—which, in fact, you do.

The number of records and the amount of information that can be stored in each record are limited mostly by the data base program. In shopping for data base management software, look for programs that can accommodate more records than you think you'll ever need. It is also quite possible that your applications will encompass more than one data base. For example, a lawyer may have client records in one data base, with another data base acting as an address book for all the colleagues, expert witnesses, judges, and associates worked with over the years. Since each data base is a separate collection and only one data base is usually searched at a time, the program needs enough power to handle as many records as the largest collection of information the lawyer would create.

Maintaining a large data base on floppy disks can be an organizational and operational challenge. If a program limits your data base to one disk, you'll suddenly have problems if the number and size of the records you need exceed that limit. Having a data base program search a floppy disk for specific records takes much longer than the same search on a hard disk. You will not have that "fingertip" feeling if you have to wait a minute or two for the computer to find and assemble the records you want from the floppy disk.

Therefore, you may want to use a hard disk if you have a large data base. Be sure to verify that your data base program can operate with a hard disk, however. Because some data base programs have built-in limitations on the number of records they handle, they can't take full advantage of all the storage space you set aside in a hard disk for data base storage. Examine this specification carefully when considering software.

Most data base management programs, including the venerable *dBASE II* (Ashton-Tate), work without difficulty with 128K of RAM installed in the computer. In fact, some programs can't take advantage of extra RAM installed. Because you are usually in one of three modes for some time—entering/editing information, searching/sorting, or printing a report—there is little advantage to transferring the program to an electronic disk. The only time that would help is when you switch from one mode to another.

Like word processing, data base management is almost exclusively text oriented. A high-resolution monochrome display is the preferred monitor, especially during long sessions in front of the computer.

Which printer you choose (if you need a printout of your data) will depend largely on how you plan to design your output forms. Try to envision the way you want a report to look when you search for a particular item. You may need a printer capable of 132-column print if the reports are going to have a lot of information printed across the page. Whether you choose a dot matrix or fully formed character printer depends upon who will be reviewing the reports and how important the look of a report is.

Telecommunications

Telecommunications (or, simply, communications) may seem like something that only large companies need to use. Telecommunications does link many field offices to corporate headquarters halfway around the globe, but it also puts people in touch with one another as well as with a variety of information services.

At the PC level, telecommunications software turns an otherwise isolated machine into one capable of sending and receiving computer information—word processing documents, reports from spreadsheet and data base management programs, and so forth—over the telephone lines (also by radio in some specialized applications). In concert with a number of services that exist today, a telecommunicating PC can send electronic mail to other computers, retrieve information from commercial data bases, and even receive software programs from free services called electronic bulletin boards. Although all these services are open to the public, commercial data bases charge for connect time—the amount of time you stay on the line to use them—as well as a subscription fee.

For most public services, you need little more inside your PC than the 64K or 128K of RAM required by the telecommunications program and a floppy disk drive on which you can store the information that will come in too fast to read. A modem is essential, of course (see Chapter 7).

In some instances, information retrieval from a large commercial data base may require the capacity of a hard disk. If you will be doing extensive research on a professional data base such as the Dialog Information Service (a collection of more than 200 specialized data bases) or Lexis (a sophisticated legal reference library), the amount of data you are likely to retrieve in any one session might exceed the capacity of a floppy disk. You could thus fill up the disk while in the middle of receiving data (*downloading*). Because the data base computer can't determine that your disk is full, you'll have to stop the transmission, change disks, and restart the download—a costly proposition on some of the expensive data base services. But by downloading onto a hard disk, you are not likely to fill up the disk.

One other application of telecommunications enables you to turn your computer into a host computer—the one other computers call. A regional manager can place the PC in the host mode overnight, for example. Traveling salespeople can call in at their convenience and get messages left for them, or send in orders gathered during the day. Traveling business people can use their portable computers to call into their offices in the evening and leave instructions for their assistants to read the next morning. A PC set up as a host computer is precisely what many of the free bulletin boards are. But if the host computer is likely to receive many data transmissions, a hard disk may be essential; otherwise, the floppy disk could fill up at 2 a.m. when no one is there to replace it.

Using your PC to communicate with a private corporate computer takes considerably more in the way of communications hardware and software than simply connecting with a data base service or a bulletin board. Most mainframe computers have very specific requirements about how the remote computers dialing into them should behave. If this is an important application for you, check with your company's data processing department or telecommunications expert before buying a computer to make sure that the add-ons your central computer requires are available for the machine you have in mind. Not all specialized communications boards or software work with all the PC compatibles.

Networking—hooking more than one computer into a group called a *local area network (LAN)*—also usually requires the guidance of someone technically adept in computer-to-computer communications. LANs are becoming popular in offices, because they allow many PC users to share costly resources such as hard disks, storage, sophisticated software, and printers. They also enable computers to function as message terminals within an office. The variety of hardware and software for networks is beyond the scope of this book, however.

Graphics
Business graphics is one of the biggest growth areas in PC software and hardware, as independent developers explore new productivity roles for the PC. The kinds of graphics tasks most often used in

business are called *presentation graphics.* This category of applications includes the graphs and charts used to create overhead projector transparencies and 35mm slides.

Without the computer, most presentation graphics are done by hand. Graphs for overhead transparencies are drawn with pen and ink, and sometimes overlaid with sections of what looks like colored cellophane. Color slides are produced by photographing a hand-made chart or graph. With a computer, all this can be done without lifting a pencil.

Graphics programs can prompt you for information about a particular graph or chart, including title, labels, and increments for X and Y axes, values to be charted, and colors to be used. The computer automatically pulls the data together into a full-color chart or graph on a color monitor. If you need a transparency, the program can direct a plotter (a mechanical drawing device) to draw on a blank transparency using colored pens. For color slides, you can attach a special photography kit to the color monitor that holds a 35mm camera in place and blocks out surrounding light while you shoot a slide of the image on the monitor.

For higher resolution graphs, some companies now offer complete hardware-software systems consisting of a separate high-resolution color monitor, a 35mm camera mount, a high-resolution graphics adapter board, and software to run the whole operation. One such system from Polaroid features the company's instant-developing 35mm color film that produces finished color slides in a matter of minutes. In business presentations, the ability to make last-minute changes on professional-looking color slides can be important.

System requirements for business graphics are generally not very rigid. Most programs require either 64K or 128K of RAM, a color monitor, and a color/graphics board. If you need a printout, you can add a plotter (which will affect your serial/parallel port availability) or one of the new ink jet color printers (if your software supports them).

Some new graphics programs make use of a light pen. If you want to use a light pen with the PC, you will need the IBM Color/Graphics Adapter and a color monitor. Because the adapter has a connector for a light pen, you will not have to use a slot for an extra board to operate it.

Integrated Software

Programs such as *1-2-3* integrate a few applications into one package, generally by limiting some of their features. But some newer, more substantial packages integrate more applications or more complete operations into one program. It is not uncommon to see spreadsheet, word processing, data base management, and graphics in one program. *MBA* (Context Management Systems) was the first such program for the PC, but today it has many challengers, including *Symphony* (Lotus Development) and *Ovation* (Ovation).

Integrated software packages have recently evolved into two groups. One group, best exemplified by *Visi On* (VisiCorp) is not composed of integrated programs per se. *Visi On* is more of a shell or a hub around which a number of independent modules revolve; it is often called an *operating environment.* When you buy *Visi On,* you really aren't buying any applications. You must add modules for the applications you want, such as *Visi On Word* for word processing. You can easily swap data from one module to another, and the different applications appear in different windows on the screen, but the system lacks the feel of integration that you might expect. One advantage of this shell idea, however, is that other software developers can license *Visi On* from VisiCorp to produce their own modules. If a wide enough variety of modules become available, you'll be able to tailor your system to the specific applications programs you want. Other more closely integrated packages aren't as open to new additions.

The other group of programs, more accurately labeled "integrated software packages," not only combine several programs into one, but often enable you to display a memo, a pie chart, and a small spreadsheet on the same screen in separate windows. As you change a figure in the spreadsheet, for example, the pie chart sections change, and a reference in the memo to the total figure also changes before your eyes. Now that's integration! *Jack2* (Business Solutions) is an example of highly integrated software.

Both types of integrated packages usually require at least 256K of RAM and a hard disk. Even if a hard disk is not required, it is still the best storage medium for this type of program. Choosing a monitor depends largely on the intended program; some require a color monitor (color/graphics board needed), while other programs that produce simpler graphics displays (simple bar charts) can be used with a monochrome monitor.

Business Applications

Even if you come to computing with the intention of doing only one application, you are bound to discover some new uses for the computer. If you can make allowances for growth early in the game, you will be better prepared to make the changes in your system without having to undo some costly hardware mistakes.

If you do a lot of word processing, for example, be aware that you will eventually have to telecommunicate a document to an editor, a business associate across the country, or your boss in the next county. In fact, it's a safe bet that for every business productivity application you have for the computer, you will someday add telecommunications capabilities to the machine. It may be via telephone to a public data base, a link to a mainframe, or a local area network within your office.

Because telecommunications will soon become a regular part of most work, try to keep one slot open for that capability. If you end up telecommunicating by telephone, you may not need the slot, provided that you have an extra serial port available on one of the expansion boards you've installed, but for networking and mainframe connections, you will probably need the slot for a special communications board.

If you are a self-employed professional who uses graphics or word processing programs in your work, you will eventually want to start doing your accounting on the computer. Even if you hire an outside accountant, you still have to organize your expenses and income so that he or she can make sense of the scraps of paper and the receipts that you gather during the year. The graphics user who has relied on a plotter as a printing device will need to add at least an inexpensive dot matrix printer to the PC system to produce a hard copy of expense data for accounting purposes.

New owners of two-floppy-disk-drive systems who get involved with many different applications should try to keep one slot open for the addition of a hard disk. You'll need the slot for the hard disk controller, whether the disk itself goes inside the System Unit or is a stand-alone subsystem. Even if you don't add a hard disk for another couple of years, if you don't plan carefully, you will probably fill up the System Unit by then.

Entertainment and Education

Using the PC at home for entertainment and education can burden a computer that was originally purchased to handle business-type applications. The problem is not in disk drives, because most entertainment and education programs need only one disk drive. The problem, as always, is in expansion slots.

Let's say you have an IBM PC with two floppy disk drives, the Monochrome Display and the appropriate adapter board, and a multifunction memory board. That leaves two slots open. If you want to use the PC for entertainment software, you are sure to need a color monitor (and the Color/Graphics Adapter) and a game controller board (although you can buy a multifunction board that contains a game controller). In one swoop, you will have filled up the

System Unit's expansion slots. Forget about adding an internal modem or a hard disk. If you limit the fun stuff to educational software, you can probably get by without a game controller board, since most educational software uses the keyboard as an input device.

The potential for sophisticated technologies being incorporated into PC-standard computers is enormous. Try to plan your computer system and its uses so that you allow for flexibility in the future, and you'll ensure a long, healthy, and productive relationship with your PC or compatible.

Essential Software Terms

Applications software	A classification of computer programs designed for specific tasks, such as word processing, data base management, or accounting.
Communications program	Software that controls the process of transferring data from one computer to another.
Data base program	Software that controls assembly, storage, and manipulation of varied information in a structured format.
Disk emulator	A portion of the computer's memory that is programmed to emulate a disk drive. It is also called an electronic disk or RAM disk.
Integrated software	A collection of two or more programs that operate interdependently, can share data, and can usually run without the need for changing disks.
Spreadsheet program	Software that manipulates data in a ledger-style format and performs calculations from formulas stored in cells of the electronic "sheet."
Utilities	Programs that manage data operations and storage within the computer and on disks. DOS is a collection of utilities.
Word processing program	Software designed for entry, manipulation, and printing of text.

CHAPTER TWELVE

PC Compatibility

Because of the success of the IBM PC, many manufacturers have created a variety of look-alikes. These companies reasoned that if one computer could become so popular, others that looked and acted like the original PC (and sometimes sold at lower prices) could also succeed. Compatibles are designed to run the same programs, accept disks and information recorded with the PC, and in some cases, use the same plug-in boards and peripherals. These computers are said to be compatible with the PC because, to varying degrees, they can run the same programs and can easily exchange information with the PC.

You can't open a computer magazine or walk into a computer store these days without encountering a PC compatible. At first, being able to choose among a dozen or more computers may sound like a great idea. In reality, however, not all claims of PC compatibility are accurate. And legally, a computer can never be a 100 percent perfect copy of the original IBM PC.

Whether your final choice is an IBM product or a compatible depends largely upon how the compatibility issue affects the work you intend to do with your computer. Your choice will also play a role in the future applications for which you may use the computer.

Compatibility Background

During the first year that IBM delivered the PC to its original network of dealers, the surge of industry interest in the machine was immense. Software translation (from 8-bit computers) and development (for the 16-bit PC) raced ahead at great speed. More development—of both software and plug-in boards—was under way for the PC than for any other computer. Demand for the PC almost always outstripped supply, despite IBM's efforts to bolster manufacturing capacity.

Because IBM wanted to bring the PC to market quickly after deciding to offer such a machine, the computer was constructed using readily available electronic components. There was nothing *proprietary*—custom designed and protected by IBM patents—about the hardware. So any knowledgeable engineer could assemble a computer using similar parts. And if that engineer found flaws in the PC, he or she could try to build a similar computer with those flaws corrected, or perhaps with enhanced features that IBM had not incorporated into the PC. Some engineers discovered that by changing the hardware design slightly (leaving out one or two expansion slots, or substituting plastic for metal components), they could even charge a little less for the computer.

In November 1982, a little more than a year after IBM shipped the first PCs to dealers, several PC-compatible computers were displayed at trade shows. There were three basic types: portables priced in the vicinity of a similarly equipped IBM desktop machine; a desktop configuration at a lower price, perhaps with some applications software included (or bundled); and either portable or desktop machines with some advanced technology and high-priced enhancements, such as a flat panel display and bubble memory. The first PC compatibles had arrived.

To many people in the industry, IBM PC's de facto standard has raised the issue of whether the existence of such a standard stifles the innovation of smaller companies. Although a standard may deter an innovator who has an excellent idea and too few dollars to launch a nonconforming product, the PC-compatible market has provided an opportunity for many entrepreneurs. Despite IBM's dominant position, there are still opportunities for engineers to develop a better machine.

Reviewers and customers began testing various manufacturers' compatibility claims by running software designed for the PC on these look-alike computers. It soon became well known that PC compatibility makes a good advertising claim, but it doesn't always hold true when you slip a PC program disk into a compatible's disk drive.

To avoid being accused of making false claims, some computer manufacturers began to use different terminology to classify the degree of compatibility their computers had with the IBM PC. Some were called 8088 compatible, meaning they used the same microprocessor as the PC. Other manufacturers claimed MS-DOS compatibility—that is, that their computers ran essentially the same disk operating system as the IBM PC. But neither compatibility claim assures that the compatible will accept software or plug-in boards designed for the PC.

Some computers are more compatible with the IBM PC than others. A few models use the 8088 microprocessor and run MS-DOS, but don't claim to be PC compatible. All MS-DOS computers, however, seem to be lumped together as PC compatibles.

MS-DOS and PC Compatibility

As noted elsewhere in this book, PC-DOS is simply IBM's version of Microsoft's MS-DOS operating system for the 8088 microprocessor. The operating system acts like a converter. If a program needs to display a character on the screen, for example, it passes an instruction that the operating system understands, no matter which computer model the program is running on. The operating system then instructs the computer to take the desired action—displaying a character in this case. If it weren't for the operating system, a different version of the program would have to be written for each computer model on the market, because the precise instructions for displaying that character are different on almost every machine.

Programs written to be compatible with MS-DOS computers are written or compiled so that they use instructions that all MS-DOS computers can understand. If you see a program you want and it is labeled for MS-DOS but not for any particular computer brand, it should work on your computer (barring any disk drive incompatibility, which is a rare occurrence). Few of the popular titles are designed for the generic MS-DOS, however; most are sold for specific computers.

One reason for the small amount of generic MS-DOS software is the limitation MS-DOS places on programmers who want to use the special features of a particular computer. To take advantage of a unique aspect of a certain computer (such as extra function keys, special video display characteristics, and so on), the programmer must add extra components to the program to augment the basic MS-DOS features.

Software that makes extensive use of the PC's special software in ROM (the BIOS) is usually labeled as being designed specifically for the IBM PC or XT. Occasionally, the software publisher adds to the label a list of those PC compatibles that have been proven compatible enough to run the software. Among the compatibles most often included on this list are the Compaq and the Columbia desktop and portable computers.

Be careful in selecting software for computers claiming PC compatibility, especially for those that are not as compatible as the Compaq or the Columbia. It is quite possible that programs written for the PC will work with computers that are less compatible, but a lot depends upon how closely the compatible's ROM BIOS replicates the PC's ROM BIOS. And exact replication is increasingly difficult, because this must be done by the compatible manufacturer without infringing on IBM's software copyright as well as the copyrights of Compaq, Columbia, and makers of other compatibles already on the market.

Most PC-compatible manufacturers publish frequently updated lists of IBM PC software that operates with their systems. Be sure to use these guides when looking at compatibles, because these guaranteed listings tell you more than you can observe by putting in a disk at the store and turning on the computer. Often, the incompatibility of software and hardware doesn't surface until you are actually using a program. Just because a computer can load a program and display the main menu or an introductory message on the monitor doesn't mean that the program and the computer are fully compatible. The program must also be able to perform its sophisticated functions, as designed, as well as read and write disks and use the printer, before it can be classified as genuinely compatible with this new computer.

An MS-DOS computer that does not claim PC compatibility is a special case. By taking the incompatibility route, manufacturers of these computers have their work cut out for them in attracting buyers. Without the ability to run the broad base of existing PC-designed software, these computer manufacturers must rely on obtaining a large enough following to make it worthwhile for third-party software developers to modify popular programs for their machines.

The inability of these machines to run PC software may stem from a different disk drive format (larger capacity or smaller disk size than the PC) or different video display techniques that can't be addressed by PC software. By and large, the companies betting on this "Lone Ranger" approach have been bearing the burden of software adaptations.

One example is the Texas Instruments Professional Computer, supplied in desktop and portable configurations. Although the company claims no PC compatibility, the TI Professional is an MS-DOS computer in a hardware configuration resembling that of the IBM PC. It runs a number of MS-DOS programs, and even a handful of PC-specific titles without modification. Thus, within a year of its formal introduction, the TI Professional had a substantial library of titles that duplicated popular PC software, most of them sold under the Texas Instruments imprint.

Manufacturers of portable computers, such as the MS-DOS Gavilan, which uses 3½-inch microfloppy disk drives, must make software available for its users in that format. No one would be able to load a program from a 5¼-inch disk into a Gavilan unless the manufacturer offered a specially designed 5¼-inch disk drive as an accessory. Even then, regular MS-DOS software wouldn't be able to take advantage of the Gavilan's unique touch-panel pointing device or special function keys. Thus, Gavilan must not only adapt existing programs, but also publish them in the new disk format.

When hardware designs wander far from the beaten path of PC compatibility, the likelihood that MS-DOS and PC software will operate successfully diminishes. When you buy a not-quite-compatible computer, you are primarily dependent on the manufacturer to keep adding new and popular programs to its software catalog. You can only hope that the company will stay in business long enough to develop a large customer base and attract independent software developers.

MS-DOS is a kind of umbrella under which a number of PC-compatible and incompatible 8088-based computers operate. Software written for a generic MS-DOS computer will operate on the PC, on most computers in standard hardware configurations claiming compatibility, and on any other standard hardware computer running MS-DOS. Software designed for the IBM PC is not guaranteed to work on every PC-compatible without prior testing. One program may work on only a few compatibles, while another program may operate flawlessly on them all. Software written specifically for the non-IBM computers—compatible or otherwise—is also available. Some of this software may run on the PC, but because it is machine specific, it's not guaranteed to run on any computer other than its own.

Degrees of Compatibility

As noted, two machines, each claiming PC compatibility, can be widely divergent in the amount of PC software they can run successfully. To better understand this, let's create an ideal PC compatible and examine the components that make it so compatible.

The ideal machine—hypothetically, 100 percent PC compatible—is built from parts purchased off the shelf from component suppliers. In every respect it is functionally identical to the IBM PC, except for the nameplate. For the finishing touch, we need to add a ROM BIOS to get the computer to act like an IBM PC. We look up the assembly language program listing for the ROM in the *IBM PC Technical Reference* manual, purchased at an IBM dealer. Then we copy the instructions bit by bit from the ROM BIOS and the PC's built-in Cassette BASIC language to make a set of ROM chips for our computer. The result—a 100 percent IBM PC-compatible computer. The only problem with this hypothetical machine is that it violates copyright laws and can never actually be sold. The law stops you from creating a perfectly compatible machine, because IBM holds proprietary rights to the instructions in ROM.

To offer a computer that will run as much PC software as possible, we hire a genius programmer who studies the IBM PC ROM BIOS listing and finds ways to change the program just enough to avoid copyright violations. The redesigned BIOS responds properly to just about everything that an applications program is likely to do. And we decide to omit the BASIC language in ROM, because customers can get the same BASIC by purchasing Microsoft's GW BASIC.

Two computers that meet this level of compatibility are those from Compaq and Columbia. A number of other machines claiming compatibility fall into this group of hardware-identical machines, with differences only in the ROM BIOS, but they are not as successful in replicating the IBM PC BIOS and thus do not run all the same software.

Next, we decide to put some improvements to the PC into our new compatible. We offer several different models that have enhancements of various PC features. Doing this enables us to please the people who find flaws in the PC. The first change is in the disk drives, because we want to scale the machine down into a more compact package. One way to use less space is to use smaller disk drives. Instead of the 5¼-inch minifloppy disk drives, we use 3½-inch microfloppy disk drives. Because PC software is not readily available on the smaller disks, we'll have to arrange with suppliers to copy their programs onto the small disks, and we'll offer the programs either with the computer (as one bundled package) or as a separate 3½-inch disk library under our brand name. Also we include an RS-232C connector built into the computer to allow users to transfer data from another MS-DOS computer. Into this compatibility category fall computers such as the Gavilan and the British-made Apricot.

Another model we introduce is a PC compatible that uses an LCD screen for a sleek, portable version. (LCD stands for liquid crystal display, similar to that of a calculator; the Gavilan is an example of a computer that uses an LCD screen.) Unfortunately, the display doesn't have the same number of lines as the PC's monitor, nor does the LCD's pixel arrangement correspond closely enough to the PC's to offer users the full PC graphics character set. If we're lucky, we can build in a special routine that intercepts PC program instructions for the screen and translates them for our screen. We'll also have several software packages converted, just in case.

Another enhancement we can make to our PC compatible is to provide more expansion slots for PC-compatible plug-in boards. The easiest way to accomplish this is to include a parallel port and one or two serial ports on the computer's System Board and bring their connectors out to the rear panel, eliminating the need for plug-in boards to provide these ports. Thus, an extra expansion slot is now available, even though two still must be reserved for the disk drive controller and the monitor adapter.

Many compatibles provide built-in parallel and serial ports. The Eagle PC Plus series, for example, has one parallel and two serial connectors built into the computer. Of the four expansion slots inside the computer, two are left free once the monitor and disk drive boards are installed.

PC or PC Compatible?

The question you may be asking at this point is whether you should consider a PC compatible (which uses the same disks and much of the same software as the PC), one of the MS-DOS compatibles (which use modified software and may have different hardware features, such as disk drives or monitor), or just buy an IBM. With MS-DOS computers that don't claim PC compatibility, you have to look closely at the available software and the reliability of the company that makes the machine. The two standouts in this category are currently the Texas Instruments Professional Computer and the Tandy TRS-80 2000. Neither machine claims PC compatibility, but both have attractive features. The TI Professional has excellent color graphics resolution and a number of sophisticated enhancements, including a telephone management system (employing state-of-the-art voice synthesis and recognition technologies) and a natural language environment (also using voice recognition) that incorporates advances in artificial intelligence research. The TRS-80 2000 also has outstanding color graphics capabilities as well as high-capacity disk drives (up to 1.4 megabytes combined) and greater processing speed over the 8088 microprocessor (it uses the newer Intel 80186 microprocessor).

The TI Professional has been on the market about a year longer than the TRS-80 2000, and about 100 programs were available upon its introduction. Since then, nearly every major program written for the IBM PC has been converted to the TI machine. Software development for the TRS-80 2000 will take longer to get going, but Tandy has the resources to build a decent library.

When considering computers that are MS-DOS compatible, you must decide whether the software currently available for the computer suits your needs and whether the company will be around long enough to support the conversion of new IBM PC software to its system. The TI and Tandy computers satisfy both of these criteria.

Choosing a more IBM-compatible PC, oddly enough, may be a greater gamble in the long run. You want the computer to perform the work you presently have, but even though such machines have the software you need today, there is always the possibility that you won't be able to use future IBM PC software with your PC compatible. Because IBM has such a large installed base of PCs, for better or worse, as IBM goes, so goes the industry. Although today there is a welcome standard among IBMs and compatibles by way of the MS-DOS operating system, IBM could provide its own operating system, one that depends so much on PC-specific ROM software that only a copyright-infringing ROM could emulate it. If that happens, and the software community, attracted by the millions of PCs already installed around the world, races to fill the applications catalog with programs tailored for that operating system, MS-DOS might be abandoned by software developers. (Of course, all the existing programs for compatibles would still operate, even if those programs become increasingly obsolete.)

Rumors that IBM will release its own operating system have been circulating for some time. Such a development may not affect machines at the XT level and below, but rather be a part of a new family of higher performance, higher priced office computers. The possibility of a new IBM operating system can't be ignored, however. If you decide to buy a PC compatible, be prepared to get as much enjoyment and productivity out of it with existing software and the features provided. Every day that your machine remains compatible with the mainstream PC, consider it a bonus. If the programs you use today are beneficial, they will also be beneficial two years or five years from now. You can only hope that your computer—and its manufacturer—will be able to adapt to new programs and new concepts that come along.

One benefit of choosing a PC-compatible computer is that you are not dependent on the survival of that computer's manufacturer to assure a steady stream of applications software in the years to come. You do, however, want to buy from a manufacturer that will stay in business to provide service and parts for your computer. An important guideline to observe in your search is to avoid buying a compatible computer via mail order from a new company.

Today, established dealers are looking for only those computer lines that stand a chance of surviving. The difference between an established dealer (or established franchise) and an inexperienced dealer is that because the newcomer probably has difficulty getting the better brands (they've already been acquired by established dealers in the area), he or she must take whatever is left, including machines from underfinanced start-up companies. Also, the established dealer may already have had bad experiences with less-than-reliable suppliers (now former suppliers) and by now knows how to weed them out before they ever get their products into the store.

Finally, let's consider the IBM PC itself. Yes, there is safety in buying a computer with the IBM logo on the panel. When new software is produced for an MS-DOS type of computer, you can be sure that it will appear in a version for the IBM PC and XT. That fact alone is incentive enough for many buyers to consider nothing but IBM.

There are drawbacks, however. Working through dealers to get answers from IBM can be frustrating, compared with a PC-compatible manufacturer that offers a toll-free phone number for help with questions or problems. You may also be annoyed by little things, such as the position of the left shift key on the PC keyboard or the lack of a built-in monitor adapter, when many compatibles have corrected those problems. But the fact remains that if you own an IBM PC, you can be reasonably certain that software and hardware will always be available and compatible with your computer. No matter how useful and compatible other manufacturers' computers may be today, a small cloud of doubt about future compatibility always hangs over them.

So far this discussion has proceeded as if the computer you buy today will be the one that takes you into the twenty-first century. That is unlikely. Of course, your investment should last as long as is feasible, but you might consider buying a PC-compatible—if one offers the special features or a price you prefer—with the expectation that if, in the future, a new standard from IBM or another manufacturer comes along, you will sell what you have and join the new trend. This may be a healthier attitude than feeling that you should buy an IBM machine because of what IBM might do in the future. If the Eagle PC or another compatible looks better on your desk than the IBM PC and is compatible with enough software to perform the tasks you want to accomplish, buy one.

A Compatible as a Second PC
Many people use a PC at work and want to take work home with them at night or over the weekend. For them, PC compatibility takes on a slightly different meaning. Chances are that the PC at home won't be an IBM, but a compatible that doesn't cost quite as much as the PC. But using both a PC and a compatible with the same programs can present problems.

Legally, you should not be using the program disk you use at work in your PC or compatible at home. According to standard software licenses, the program disk you buy is for use on one specific machine only. According to the law, if you want to use that program on your machine at home, you must buy a second copy of the program.

You must also be absolutely positive that the two computers read and write data on the disks identically. If that is not the case, the work you do at the office may not be readable in the computer you use at home, and vice versa.

If your compatible has specially designed software, such as a custom version of *WordStar,* that version and the version on your office PC will probably have to be from the same generation for the two programs to work properly on both machines. Software programs evolve, and periodic updates are produced by their publishers. Make sure that the programs you'll be using on both computers have the same version or release number (such as version 3.30 of *WordStar*). (Differing versions of the same program generally will not produce incompatible files or data, however; you can usually use the files produced by a program with a later version of that same program.)

If you want to buy a PC compatible as a second computer, take copies of your data disks from the office when you shop. Run the corresponding programs on the dealer's compatible and read and write information to the disks. Also write files on a blank disk using the compatible's programs. Then take the disks back to your office, and make sure that the new files on both your data disks and the new one you made at the store work perfectly with your software. If all the data is completely readable, you have a disk and a program match, and that PC-standard machine is a safe buy for those applications.

Compatibles and BASIC Programs

As noted previously, a large part of the Advanced BASIC language in the PC is supplied in the computer's ROM. This is an important factor to consider if you plan to use your compatible with PC programs written in BASIC, such as many educational programs and those published as listings in magazines.

With the IBM PC, if you want to run an Advanced BASIC program or learn how to program in BASIC, you simply load the Advanced BASIC from the DOS disk before loading the program. But in PC compatibles, there is no BASIC language in ROM or on the DOS disk. To run BASIC on them, you need BASIC in disk form. Most of the compatibles offer GW BASIC (you can also get a generic MS-DOS version), which was developed by Microsoft. GW BASIC is essentially identical to IBM Advanced BASIC, also called BASICA.

Compatible Catalog

In the fast-changing business of PC compatibles, attempting to catalog all the available models is risky. Features change, old models go and new models come, degrees of compatibility change, prices go in both directions, and the selection of software bundled with the computers changes frequently.

Acknowledging all that can go wrong in such a listing, we present PC-standard computers from 18 manufacturers. Most of the manufacturers claim some degree of PC compatibility. This listing should give you an idea of the compatibles in the marketplace; because the features and models of these computers can change rather frequently, the machines described here are intended to be representative of PC-standard computers. Be sure to check and compare the details of all machines you are considering before making a final selection. (A detailed discussion of PC-standard computers appears in *PC World* magazine, April 1984.)

Bytec   The Hyperion from Bytec-Comterm is one of the most attractive PC compatibles on the market. It is a relatively lightweight portable that has two disk drives, a built-in amber monitor, and a built-in modem. The company also makes a matching expansion chassis that contains seven PC-compatible expansion slots, but there is no room for expansion within the Hyperion itself. In recent tests, the Hyperion failed to work with a number of PC software products. But because PC compatibility levels change from time to time, you might try this machine on software you want to run before closing the door on this well-made computer. (Distributor Anderson-Jacobson also sells this computer under the brand name Passport.)

Columbia   A manufacturer whose products consistently rank high in PC hardware and software compatibility is Columbia Data Products, which makes three models: the portable VP and two desktop MPC models, one with two floppy disk drives, one with a hard disk and one floppy disk drive. Columbia has priced these systems attractively and includes enough bundled software to keep you reading owner's manuals for months. The desktop models offer color graphics, while the portable provides only monochrome graphics.

Compaq   If we were to rank compatible computers, the Compaq would be at the top. The Compaq is the first PC compatible to capture a meaningful share of the PC market. In dozens of tests and reviews by magazines and consultants, the Compaq has performed consistently as the most compatible PC on the market. There is very little software that Compaq computers don't run.

The Compaq and Compaq-Plus are portable machines featuring a built-in high-resolution green screen that displays graphics. The Compaq comes with one double-sided 5¼-inch disk drive and has room for a second drive (recommended), while the Compaq-Plus comes with one floppy disk drive and one of the best shock-mounted 10-megabyte hard disk drives in the industry.

Corona   The Corona PC and Portable PC were among the first PC compatibles to arrive on dealer shelves. Although they come with bundled software, the selection is not quite as extensive as that of the Columbia. You get MS-DOS, GW BASIC, *PC Tutor,* and *MultiMate,* a sophisticated word processing program. The desktop PC can be configured with two double-sided floppy disk drives, or one hard disk and one floppy disk drive. The portable is available with only one or two floppy disk drives.

Eagle   The PC-compatible computers from Eagle have changed considerably since they were first offered. Today, Eagle offers remarkably compatible desktop and portable computers; both are available with a hard disk, if desired. The Eagles are known for their crisp monochrome displays, quiet desktop operation, and sensible desktop model styling that enables you to tuck the keyboard out of the way when it is not in use. The Eagles are definitely worth investigating, but buy only from a dealer who offers full service and is knowledgeable.

Gavilan   In the briefcase category of MS-DOS compatible machines is the Gavilan. Offered in two styles, with either 8 or 16 lines by 80 columns across the built-in LCD display, the Gavilan employs a unique touch panel that is used as a kind of pointing device. The position of your finger on the rectangular touch panel corresponds to a location on the LCD display. To keep the computer small, a 3½-inch microfloppy disk drive is built into the unit.

Gavilan now offers a 5¼-inch disk drive accessory for its portables, which lets you use IBM PC data disks with the Gavilan. The disk drive accessory can be used for data disks only; IBM PC programs cannot be loaded into the Gavilan. You can use a program, such as *WordStar,* on both machines, however, and use files from one data disk on either machine (with the auxiliary drive). The Gavilan is an attractive, well-built portable, but the skimpy selection of software for it should be a prime concern, followed by its relatively high price.

Hewlett-Packard   The HP-150 is an MS-DOS compatible computer from Hewlett-Packard, a company that has a reputation for producing high-quality, innovative electronics products. While

HP's earlier personal computer models attracted little attention, the HP-150 has caused a bit of a stir, because it is the first product of its type to use a touch screen. Instead of positioning the cursor on the screen with cursor keys or a mouse, you literally touch the screen at the exact spot you want something done.

In addition to this unusual capability, which must be specially programmed for all applications, the HP-150 uses 3½-inch microfloppy disk drives. Hewlett-Packard has already adapted a number of popular, powerful business applications programs for the computer, including *MBA* (Context Management) and *1-2-3* (Lotus Development). If consumer interest in the HP-150 is strong enough, the company is sure to adopt many new programs for the touch screen.

IBM What is IBM doing in this list, you ask? Don't forget that a recent addition to the PC family, PCjr, is a PC-compatible computer. Many people who use a PC at work are probably considering getting a PCjr for use at home. At present, the PCjr is limited to a maximum of 128K of RAM. That figure is deceiving, however, because as much as 16K of that memory must be used by the computer to control the video screen. If you have a high-powered program such as *1-2-3*, it may not run on the PCjr. Another thing to bear in mind is that the PCjr has only one disk drive. Because some PC programs perform a lot of disk accesses on a two-drive system, running those programs on the PCjr will involve so much disk swapping that work may seem counterproductive. But for many PC programs, you will be able to use the same program and data disks in both the PC and the PCjr.

ITT From corporate giant ITT comes a PC compatible called XTRA. In technical specifications, this well-engineered, professional-looking computer matches those of the IBM PC almost step for step. It is about the only PC-compatible computer that includes a mouse pointing device as standard equipment. XTRA is banking on being an early proponent of the *Microsoft Windows* operating environment, which makes use of a mouse by presenting command options on the screen with simple menus. XTRA has a significantly high degree of PC software compatibility.

Leading Edge PC Housed in a rather clumsy-looking box, the Leading Edge desktop PC features 128K of RAM, two double-sided disk drives, and a monochrome monitor. It also comes packaged with MS-DOS, GW BASIC, and *Leading Edge Word Processor*.

The Leading Edge PC's other claim to fame is that its 8088 microprocessor operates twice as fast as the 8088 used in the IBM PC and most other PC compatibles. Such speed can be an advantage on some programs that do a lot of internal processing. But because many educational and entertainment programs use the microprocessor's clock rate in critical timing functions, some of these programs will not work with the Leading Edge computer.

Panasonic   Although Japanese computer manufacturers have been trying to break into the American market, none have been particularly successful to date. Panasonic has introduced a product that could reverse that trend. The Sr. Partner is a self-contained, PC-compatible transportable computer that boasts an impressive list of compatible software. It offers 128K of RAM (expandable to 512K), one double-sided 5¼-inch disk drive (with room for an optional second drive), a 9-inch monochrome text/graphics monitor, a built-in thermal printer, and a selection of top-name software. You're limited to only one add-on board, but with built-in serial and parallel ports, you wouldn't need much more from a portable computer, except perhaps a clock/calendar board or a built-in modem.

Pronto   Another computer that employs the new 80186 microprocessor comes from Pronto Computers. Several versions of desktops and portables are available, depending on the type of disk drive and, in the case of the desktop versions, the type of monitor you want.

Pronto Computers offer a hard disk (up to 35 megabytes) or a removable cartridge hard disk with a capacity of 5.6 megabytes. The floppy disk drives on all Pronto computers are rated at 800K, with 96 tracks per inch. The machine's specifications state, however, that the drives are compatible with the PC's 48 tracks per inch. In informal tests at a trade show, however, the Pronto series failed to run a number of popular applications written for the PC. All Pronto computers come bundled with an integrated productivity software package that includes word processing, an electronic spreadsheet, and data base management.

Seequa   At the low end of the PC-compatible price scale is the Seequa Chameleon. The Chameleon is a self-contained portable computer with both the Intel 8088 and an 8-bit Z80A microprocessor. The Chameleon can run not only MS-DOS software but also CP/M software. This model comes with two single-sided disk drives and a 9-inch monochrome graphics display. The Chameleon Plus, a version of the computer that has double-sided drives, costs about $900 more. Built into the Chameleon models are a serial port, a parallel port, and a connection for a composite color monitor.

The Chameleons are compatible with a large selection of PC software. Some reviewers, however, have objected to the quality of some of the components of this budget computer. Be sure to investigate carefully if you are considering a Chameleon.

Sperry   IBM PCs have been capturing the market for desktop computers in corporations currently using mainframe computers made by other companies. Some of these companies are responding by producing personal computers that have the ability to emulate IBM PCs and communicate with various mainframes. Sperry has done just that with the Sperry Personal Computer. It uses an Intel 8088 microprocessor that operates twice as fast as the IBM PC's. You can, however, switch it down to the IBM speed if a program demands it. In addition to its IBM PC-compatible specifications, the Sperry PC offers some enhancements in higher resolution color graphics. Several configurations are available, depending on the type or types of disk drive (floppy or hard disk) and monitor (monochrome, medium-resolution color, and high-resolution color) you need. The Sperry machine is surprisingly compatible with PC software, indicating that a lot of research and development went into the design of this product.

Strategic Technologies   Another portable new to the market is Strategic Technologies' PC Traveler. This machine is an all-in-one portable housed in its own carrying case. The computer uses not one but two Intel 80186 microprocessors and has a built-in flat-panel gas plasma screen (80 columns by 25 lines), a dot matrix printer, and a choice of either a removable 6.2-megabyte cartridge hard disk drive or two 5¼-inch floppy disk drives. The computer is rated as being compatible with data disks from the PC, but its programs will have to come from another source. Investigate the availability of software for this compatible if it interests you.

Tandy   In an uncharacteristic move for Tandy (Radio Shack), the company unveiled a major computer that uses an outside operating system, MS-DOS, for its TRS-80 2000 computer. The 2000 uses the Intel 80186 microprocessor and formats its disks at 96 tracks per inch for a storage capacity of about 400K per disk. Because the machine's ability to read or write to IBM PC data disks is not guaranteed in this disk format, the machine is not completely PC compatible. In fact, Tandy makes no such claims in that direction, although Tandy provides a conversion program that transfers information from some IBM PC data disks to the Tandy format. The 2000 has an excellent dealer network—thousands of Radio Shack Computer Centers and stores. The list of available software for the machine will probably be small for some time, however. If PC compatibility is not a particularly high priority for you, keep an eye on this machine, because a number of its capabilities outdistance those of the IBM PC.

Texas Instruments   Coming from an entirely different corporate division than the company's ill-fated home computer, the TI Professional Computer and its companion portable were not intended to be PC compatible, although a number of PC programs work on the machines without modification. In addition, TI has published or arranged with original publishers to release just about every popular applications program you'd want in the TI format. Not all the programs take advantage of the TI PC's extra function keys, but the system is well built and features a number of unique enhancements in voice and telephone management that make it worth looking into if a high degree of PC compatibility is not a significant issue for you.

Visual   An unusually styled portable, the Visual Commuter features a full-sized PC-compatible keyboard and a large number of built-in features, including support for an IBM Monochrome Display and for a color monitor, a serial port, a parallel port, room for two 5¼-inch double-sided disk drives, and space for up to 512K of RAM on the system board. The computer can be used with an optional 80-column by 16-line LCD display or with the excellent IBM Monochrome Display.

A prototype of the Commuter proved largely compatible with popular PC applications software, including *WordStar* and *1-2-3*, but when it was used with a full-sized monitor, only 23 lines of text were displayed on the screen at a time (rather than the standard 24 lines).

The Future
To the old adage about the only things you can count on—death and taxes—add the development of more PC compatibles. As new display, memory, and mass storage technologies become affordable, you can be sure they'll be incorporated into new machines by manufacturers hungry for the market IBM has created. Buy with care when considering a compatible computer, however. Consider what you want the computer to do, and test its capabilities. *Compatibility* is a term that is used often but that doesn't necessarily apply to all IBM PC look-alikes.

Dealers and Maintenance Plans

Buying a personal computer has never been easy. If you've been through the process once—having purchased a home computer, for example—you know that the transaction involves many uncertainties. Which is the right computer? Are there some hidden costs in additional equipment needed to make it function like a real computer? Why can't the clerk explain the differences between a VIC-20 and an Atari 600XL?

Manufacturers of machines in the home computer category have decided that their products don't need much in the way of technical support at the point of sale. Any problems a customer may have trying to understand the machine or the software can theoretically be handled through local service centers or toll-free telephone calls to the manufacturer's technical staff. Although you may doubt the validity of that kind of thinking, such a system does assure that mass merchandisers can successfully sell a lot of computers to eager, price-conscious consumers. In all fairness to these manufacturers, their computers are by and large easy to install and, with the reliance on cartridge software, easy to use.

But the kind of computer discussed in this book is not quite as simple, especially because the IBM PC requires considerable retail assistance in assembling a functional computer. Admittedly, some PC compatibles are so self-contained that you can literally unpack the box to find a fully operational computer inside. But you still need a dealer to help with purchasing decisions. You will have questions about the computer both before and after you buy it that only a well-trained salesperson at an authorized dealer can answer correctly. And because you'll be spending anywhere from $2000 to $7000 on a system, you want to be able to trust that the dealer is giving you the right information.

With PC-standard computers, where you buy is usually as important as what you buy. If you purchase a computer in a combative or otherwise unpleasant atmosphere, your satisfaction with the system may be in jeopardy. And if your attitude toward the dealer is negative after the sale, you may be reluctant to call with questions or problems.

At the other end of the scale is the conscientious dealer who works hard to serve customers. If problems arise, this dealer not only attempts to solve them quickly, but may also suggest solutions that cost that store money, such as loaning you a printer until yours comes in. The strategy is that you will appreciate the efforts made on your behalf so much that you will come back to that store for future purchases.

Ideally, you want to establish a long-term relationship with a dealer and a salesperson at that dealership. The more the salesperson knows about you and the work you want to do with a computer, the more likely you are to receive notices about new equipment or specials at the store that might appeal to you.

This ideal in dealer service is difficult to find, however. A more common scenario may pit you against a salesperson who is more concerned with the commission he or she can earn from the sale than with matching the right system to your needs. This kind of salesperson probably does not keep notes about customers and their needs, and once you've made your purchase, you'll never get another call. It will be up to you to find out what's new. If you call with a problem about something you don't understand, you may get the distinct impression that you are intruding. After selling dozens of computers, an impatient salesperson may not be interested in hearing from someone who doesn't understand how to transfer control codes to a printer.

Shopping for a Dealer
Unless you can afford to be casual with the dollars set aside for a computer, you should visit a number of dealers in your area who handle PC-standard computers. If you live in an area that has few computer stores, you may have to either invest time and energy

going to the nearest major city to shop or be prepared to accept whatever level of service the nearest dealer provides.

IBM PCs and compatibles are sold primarily through outlets called full-service dealers. They are the opposite of the outlets known as mass merchandisers. A full-service dealer's staff consists of professional salespeople who have received technical training about the products they sell. Salespeople in a full-service store should offer to spend time with you while you are in the discovery stage, helping you match software and hardware to your intended applications. They should set up and test your system before you take it out of the store. They should also be prepared to help you with your start-up problems when you call or come to the store after buying the system, and provide software support.

There are telltale signs by which you can determine a dealer's professionalism when you shop at computer stores. The store should be clean. Stacks of boxes around the showroom floor, messy work areas where customers are to experiment with the equipment, dusty equipment, and disorganized shelves of software, books, and magazines are all signs that the store management and personnel don't care about their own environment. If you find such a store, don't expect too much attention to be paid to your own concerns. A good retailer will try to impress potential customers with a pleasant environment.

The computer systems carried by the dealer should be arranged neatly and concisely so you can focus your attention on one computer—sitting down in a comfortable chair in front of it for an hour, if necessary. If you are visually bombarded by three systems connected to seven printers and four monitors on one crowded desk, you will be unable to get a feeling for how any one system operates.

A wise dealer provides an environment that will inspire you. If a dealer is trying to sell you on the idea of a computerized office, the display area should have good lighting and be uncluttered. Miles of exposed cabling hints at the potentially confusing time you might have once you get your machine installed.

Around the display areas and elsewhere throughout the store, readily available printed information should keep you occupied if a salesperson can't get to you right away. Customer-oriented stores have signs directing you to the kind of computer you might be interested in. Such a store might have an Apple area, an IBM area, a portable computer area, and so on.

Another sign of professionalism is an area devoted to training. Although this is not a prerequisite to a good dealer, stores that have training areas and a posted schedule of classes are generally prepared to support their customers. If the salespeople conduct the classes, there is a good chance that they know about the products they sell. Not every dealer's courses are necessarily the best, however. Some are not worth the extra fees charged by the dealer. But at this point—before you buy the computer—you are looking for reliable expertise, and the salesperson who teaches classes probably has a leg up on the one who does not.

Finding the Right Salesperson

One of the worst experiences of going into a computer store with the sincere intention to learn, and perhaps buy, is being ignored by everyone who looks like a salesperson. This happens so often that it may qualify as the number one problem facing computer customers today. If you are ignored or have a bad experience at a dealership, give the salespeople a second chance. Go back on a different day of the week, and try to get the attention of someone who looks competent. If your second attempt fails to satisfy you, cross that store off your list.

When you do make contact, establish an open relationship with the salesperson. The only way you'll feel secure is if you really trust him or her. When you walk into the store, the salesperson will be trying to qualify you—to see if you are a legitimate future buyer—and figure out what kind of machine you'd be interested in. While you're being sized up, qualify the salesperson. It takes some personal chemistry to make a good relationship; what you'd like to see in a salesperson may be different from what someone else might want.

Avoid the "know-it-all" type who has heard your story before and knows exactly what you need, even before you get a chance to explain. He or she does all the talking and is really pushy. A pitch rolls off the tongue so fast that you know it's been done a thousand times before, precisely the same way. You get the feeling that you're not exactly wanted, as if he or she would rather be playing *Invaders from Gorgonzola*. Because you can never tell a know-it-all anything, don't bother trying. Just head for the exit.

When you find a salesperson who seems genuinely interested in the specifics of your intended computer application, he or she should be asking you all kinds of questions. You should be doing most of the talking on the first visit. It is unlikely that you will have fully thought out all the operations you'd like your computer to do. Don't say, "I want to do an electronic spreadsheet" or "I need word processing." Because there are so many variations to each of those applications, you will have to supply the details of your working environment if a salesperson is to tailor a hardware and software system to your needs. The salesperson who jumps to conclusions about your work without fully understanding it borders on the dreaded know-it-all. Even if he or she has heard your story a dozen times, a good salesperson will encourage you to believe that yours is unique and should be told from beginning to end. Good ears are a salesperson's most useful tools.

Once you think you've found a salesperson whom you like, it's time to find out how he or she handles technical questions. You want to make sure that the advice you will be getting is accurate and informed, but there is such an information overload about personal computers today that no single person can know it all. Hardware and software developments move so quickly that even a sincere salesperson can't know the details about every product in the store, much less other brands found in other stores.

Concomitant with this flood of information is a substantial amount of misinformation. Broad generalizations—"graphics resolution is better on this machine than all the others across the street"—tend to be thrown out at customers without study or knowledge of the specifics. Generalizations are dangerous for you but handy for the salesperson; one trite phrase can save a busy salesperson hours of study.

In testing a salesperson's knowledge, stick to the computers carried in the store. Ask some technical questions for which you already have the answers, such as the differences between serial and parallel printers, or why a hard disk for the IBM PC needs an external power supply, or the differences between a composite color monitor and RGB monitor. If the answers are associated with a detailed, nontechnical explanation, you've found a winner. If a salesperson doesn't honestly know the answer to one of your questions, he or she should admit it and try to find the answer. An answer that is contrived just to make the salesperson look omniscient is a bad sign. There is no sin in not knowing everything.

A professional salesperson knows that the odds of your buying on the first visit are slim. He or she will determine the price of a system tailored to your needs and perhaps make a printout of the results for you to take along with whatever product brochures are available. The salesperson should offer you a business card, so you can contact him or her to ask further questions or perhaps to set up an appointment for a second meeting.

Once you've settled on a dealer and a salesperson, be prepared to return two or three times before you make a purchase. At each visit, spend a half-hour or more with the computer and the software you want to use. If possible, bring along samples of the work you want to do on a computer, and experiment. Try out printers with the software you'll be using. Ask questions. Find out about maintenance charges (see the discussion of maintenance contracts later in this chapter). The best time to work with the computer is during the business day. Computer stores are usually too crowded to encourage concentration on weekends and evenings. Better yet, make an appointment with the salesperson for some before- or after-hours time with the computer.

As much as you'd like to believe that the salesperson will set you up with the best equipment and software you could buy, keep in mind that it is that person's job to sell you what the store carries. It would be foolish for the salesperson to lose out on a nice commission by directing you across town to buy a printer.

What you have to guard against is the salesperson who tries to push extra equipment on you. Your best defense is to arm yourself with knowledge about your needs and what hardware and software combination meets those needs. Don't expect the salesperson to do unbiased research for you.

After-Sale Support

Although before-sale assistance and after-sale support are the extras for which you'll pay higher than discount prices, some customers do abuse the privilege, especially after the sale. At times, the dealer is caught in the middle between a demanding customer and an inflexible support system from hardware and software manufacturers.

For many products sold through computer stores, the dealer is the customer's only recourse for questions or problems. Too many hardware and software manufacturers pass support for their products onto dealers, instead of offering telephone assistance. One reason for this is, of course, the cost of both the support staff and the toll-free phone calls that would have to be borne by the manufacturer. But another reason is that if there is a lot of repetition in questions from customers, the dealer already has the answers handy and can solve the problem on a local level more efficiently than if the manufacturer answered those questions individually.

This is not true, of course, for the problem or the question that the dealer has not previously encountered. For such help, dealers have their own hot-line numbers (usually toll-free) to manufacturers. The dealer may have difficulty reaching the right people to get a speedy reply to a technical question. Once the answer comes in, there is further delay until it reaches you. Some of the biggest names—especially IBM—use this support method. But until they improve their system, we will have to live with delays and inefficiencies. Both the customer and the dealer are caught in the middle much of the time.

As a customer of a full-service dealer, you are entitled to a computer system—hardware and software—that runs as promised. Because the system should perform the tasks you want in the way the dealer said it would, it is important that you work with actual examples of your work at the store before buying. The more specific you are about the system you need, the more responsible the dealer will be to make sure that it works for you.

In the search for the ever-elusive bargain, some shoppers piece their systems together from several dealers—a computer here, disk drives there, a printer way over there, and software from out back. Although buying in that manner may save you a few hundred dollars, you may also find yourself in an agonizing bind if something goes wrong with any of the components. This is especially true because problems with computers have a mysterious way of being difficult to track down. Let's say you are having some trouble, such as difficulty in making the printer work with the software. Your nightmare begins when you take the system to what would seem like the most logical dealer for warranty repair. The dealer will look at the system and notice that he or she did not sell you some of the components, nor does the dealer know how the program and printer work, since that store doesn't stock those brands. The dealer will likely conclude that your problem must be with one of the other components. Trips to each of the other dealers will probably get the same response. If you spread your system purchase across several dealers, no one is likely to take responsibility for problems. Each dealer may attest to the quality and the proper operation of the piece purchased there. But you're stuck if those pieces refuse to function as a unit.

The only way to avoid this problem is to buy the major components of your system from one dealer. This kind of purchase may be more costly initially, but you will probably save money in the long run. Most dealers guarantee that the systems they sell will work as specified. Some dealers, including Sears Business Systems Centers, even go as far as guaranteeing your satisfaction or your money back.

Avoid the Fly-by-Nighter
Within the past couple of years, a few stories have surfaced about authorized dealers of major brands of computers running off with deposits from their customers without delivering the goods. Of course, computer dealers aren't the only culprits in this kind of scam, but when computers are in high demand and short supply, as is the case with many new models, buyers are willing to do almost anything to guarantee a spot on the waiting list.

Authorized dealers of major brand computers are scrutinized rather closely by manufacturers to ensure that the retailers have the means and the management to maintain an ongoing business. Generally speaking, a store that has qualified as an IBM or Apple dealer is a good bet.

Although the retail computer business is relatively young, some independent dealers have been around since the late 1970s, have survived the worst of times, and are good candidates for dependable service. New, independent stores may be less reliable. The trend with new stores these days is the franchise. In addition to familiar names such as ComputerLand and CompuShop, several well-financed franchises are surfacing in communities around the country. Dealers who have substantial corporate backing, such as IBM Product Centers and Sears Business Systems Centers, are also safe bets.

If you want to reserve a machine that is temporarily out of stock, a respectable dealer will ask for a deposit of no more than 10 to 15 percent of the purchase price. Avoid the dealer who demands the full price as a deposit. That dealer is either underfinanced or unprofessional.

Retail vs. Mail-Order Shopping

The desire to save a few dollars on a computer system is a strong one. If you've looked through computer magazines, you've surely seen one- and two-page advertisements of discounters offering low prices, a toll-free telephone-ordering number, and convenient credit card payment. You won't find many IBM PCs advertised this way because IBM does not authorize such dealers, but you will see PC compatibles and every possible hardware accessory imaginable. Your temptation, then, may be to milk a local dealer for support and guidance before the sale, and then buy as much as you can from a discount supplier.

If you're a newcomer to PC-standard computers, this is not a good plan. One of the things you're not paying for when you buy from most mail-order discounters is the after-sale support you will need as a novice. If getting help from a dealer before you buy many of your components from the mail-order supplier is difficult, forget trying to get help after you buy elsewhere. The dealer is under no obligation to answer questions or perform warranty service for you.

The mail-order suppliers have their place in this bustling PC market, however. If you have friends who, based on their experience, recommend particular plug-in boards or software and are ready to help you if you run into problems, you can save money by purchasing extras from a mail-order discounter. The gamble you take is that unless the product is damaged, the mail-order dealer is under no obligation to take it back if it doesn't do what the manufacturer's advertisements and magazine reviews led you to believe.

Component	Cost of 9-Month Contract
PC System Unit	$150
PC XT System Unit (excluding hard disk)	$175
10-megabyte fixed disk	$142
Monochrome Display	$ 35
Color Monitor	$ 75
Graphics Printer	$ 42

Figure 13.1 *A summary of typical costs for a 9-month maintenance contract for IBM PC components.*

Once you get more experience with your PC, the mail-order discounter will play a bigger role in software and hardware add-on purchases.

Of course, you won't get the personal treatment from a mail-order supplier that you can get from the local retail dealer. If you buy from a dealership, drop in from time to time to renew the relationship. Bring your salesperson up to date on what you've been doing with your system. Find out what's new in the store. Check out the bookshelves for the latest titles in your specialty area. Eventually—years down the road, perhaps—you will be buying another computer, and you'll need the dealer's support again.

Maintenance Contracts

When you buy your computer, chances are you will be presented with an opportunity to purchase a service contract that essentially extends your warranty. Most PCs, including IBM's, come with a 90-day warranty on parts and labor. Most dealers offer contracts for 9 months (to bring your coverage out to a full year) or 12 months beyond the original 90 days.

Because dealers offer different maintenance policies, inquire about them when you are selecting a dealer. Some dealers have established rates for maintenance contracts covering each piece of your system, or major components such as the IBM PC System Unit with one or two disk drives, the Monochrome Display, and so forth. Other dealers charge a percentage of the sales price of the entire system. Any way you look at it, a maintenance contract for an IBM PC or XT is not inexpensive. A summary of typical contract rates for IBM PC components is given in Figure 13.1. Rates for comparable systems vary from dealer to dealer.

At the dealer offering the prices listed in Figure 13.1, the costs for a 12-month contract on these components were in many cases half again as much. The PC System Unit contract went up to $225, while the Color Monitor was slightly over $110. The incremental charges are disproportionately high compared with the additional time coverage.

Other dealers price maintenance contracts according to a fixed percentage of the total purchase price of the system. This can range from 8 to 10 percent of the price for a 12-month contract (giving you a total of 15 months of warranty protection). A 12-month contract on a $3500 system would cost about $350 for the entire system.

These charges, incidentally, are for carry-in service—bringing the system to the store for repair. Some dealers promise that the machine can be repaired and ready for pickup within 24 hours, or even the same day (depending on the problem) if you get the unit into the shop early in the morning. If you want a service person to come to your location, you will have to purchase an on-site service contract—a very expensive alternative. On-site service contracts can cost 30 to 50 percent more than carry-in service. For example, an on-site contract for a $3500 system could cost from $450 to $525 per year. After the first one-year contract expires, most dealers will renew it for another year, although often at a higher rate.

If you move across the country and want to have a service contract with a local dealer, you'll have to shop around carefully for the best deal. Some dealers may not be eager to extend a contract on a system they did not sell. Others will be glad to do so, provided that you bring in the system for a checkup. That way the dealer can be assured that the system is in working condition when the contract is issued. The dealer may charge a fee—often $25 or $50—to inspect the machine.

Out-of-Warranty Repair

The value of a service contract should be measured against the cost of something going wrong with your system after the 90-day warranty ends. If you think there must be a reason for the high contract costs, you won't be disappointed. Computer service, especially for the IBM PC, can be nightmarishly expensive. Thus, a service contract could pay for itself the first time the machines goes to the shop.

A technician charges an hourly rate just to look at your machine, a cost that can range from $45 to $75 per hour, and probably higher in some metropolitan areas. That figure does not include parts, which often constitutes a major portion of the repair cost. The practice in repair centers operated by IBM and many other dealers is not to replace the faulty component, which might be a one-dollar chip or five-cent capacitor. If a component fails on the System Board, the repair technician will generally replace the entire System Board. And if your PC is out of warranty or not covered by a service contract, you have to pay for that replacement board—several hundred dollars' worth. If a double-sided floppy disk drive fails, you'll have to replace it with a new one at about $500. To that add the price of a couple of hours of labor to have a repair person track down the problem and replace the unit.

If the module-replacement method is the repair policy of your PC dealer, you should be told that when you purchase the system. Salespeople may be reluctant to tell you about such a policy, for fear that the prospect of exorbitant repairs might scare you away from buying the system from them. Unlike some other types of service contracts, you cannot compare the cost of a PC service contract against the hourly rate charged by the service technician and factor in a small percentage for parts. You'll be mistakenly led to believe that in place of a $350 service contract, you'll come out ahead by paying for a couple of hours of work at $60 an hour plus maybe another $35 in parts. In modular PC service, it's the price of parts that kills you.

The Risks

Despite the horror of potentially high repair costs, you may not want to purchase a service contract. But evaluate the risks you'll be taking if you decline that option. In your favor is the tendency of any kind of electronic device to show signs of failure early in its life. If the computer contains a faulty component, chances are that the entire system will fail immediately (in computer jargon, "dead on arrival"). Have the dealer set up your system and run the specialized diagnostics routines for 24 to 48 hours before you take the equipment home. Severe problems usually show up when you first turn on the machine. Beyond that, most other problem parts will fail or act up within the warranty period. Naturally, the longer the factory warranty, the more protection you have against the possibility of component failure. Although IBM's warranty is only 90 days, a number of PC compatibles, such as the Eagle, have one-year warranties.

The warranty period is also the time during which you are most likely to make a significant blunder that might accidentally damage the machine. If the machine wasn't well built, its weaknesses will show up during the warranty period, when you are learning your way around it.

After the factory warranty expires, any problems will most likely be in mechanical components—the disk drives and the printer. Of the two, the disk drive is more likely to need repair. As noted earlier, the floppy disk and fixed disk drives are precision mechanical instruments, and mechanical devices wear out with use. There's no telling when it will happen to your disk drives. You may own your computer for years without having a problem with the drives. Your neighbor, however, may have one fail within a month after the warranty expires—lending credence to the suspicion that some sort of timer is buried inside every computer to signal when the warranty has expired.

Calculating the Risks

Now that you have an idea of repair costs, you have to determine whether your computer is a high-risk machine. Consider a service contract a form of insurance. If your computer will be installed in a high-risk environment, the insurance offered by the service contract is well worth the cost. Unlike homeowner's or automobile insurance, however, a PC service contract doesn't take into account factors that make the computer's installation a particularly high or low risk. That's for you to decide.

If you plan to use your PC in an office environment, particularly one in which more than one person will have access to the computer, you run a high risk that something disastrous will happen to the computer. An inexperienced user may insert a disk backwards or set a file folder atop the monitor for several hours until the heat inside the cabinet destroys a small component (possibly necessitating the replacement of the entire monitor).

You might consider the risk in an office environment great enough that on-site service should prevail. If the PC plays a key role in your business, you may not have the time or the personnel to take a computer to the store and back. Evaluate the cost of the time it takes to transport the computer versus the incremental cost of an on-site service contract.

Using the PC in a one-person office represents a moderate risk. A lot depends upon the care of the user. Quite often, the person who was once a computer novice becomes so used to the machine that he or she takes it for granted. That person may put an ashtray containing a smoking cigarette or a pipe on the desk in front of the disk drives, or put a stack of papers on top of the monitor. If you fail to treat complex machinery with respect over the long term, it will respond accordingly by developing some kind of malfunction.

Whether or not a home installation of a PC calls for a service contract depends upon who uses the machine. If the kids get to it, or if the single user in the household is the careless type, a contract may be worthwhile.

Portable PCs, if they are used as portables, should be covered by a service contract if your dealer offers one. In fact, you might consider selecting a dealer for this type of machine only if he or she offers a service agreement on the portable. Disk drives are more likely to be a problem on a computer that is toted around, no matter how carefully it is handled. Just setting the computer down on a desk repeatedly can slowly loosen critical parts or jiggle some component that shouldn't be jiggled. And if the portable has a hard disk, a service contract is essential.

Make sure to get all the facts regarding the specific components and repairs covered by the agreement. Find out if the dealer attempts to repair a faulty disk drive and monitor or simply swaps these components for new ones. If the technician actually repairs the problem component—which is uncommon—the cost of a typical repair might be small enough for you to consider avoiding a contract and "self-insuring" the computer.

Essential Supplies

Before you leave the store with a computer, a modem, a printer, and software, don't forget to buy a few essential computer supplies. Blank disks and printer paper are items that you will need on a continuing basis. They are the consumables of computer use, just as food and soap products are the consumables of the household.

When you buy your computer, you will already be inundated with all kinds of boxes and intimidating new equipment. But because you'll need some basic supplies to set up your system, you may just decide to get what you need in the computer store. For this convenience, you will pay whatever price the dealer is asking.

Later, once you've settled into using your system, you can begin looking around for better prices on the goods you use up quickly. Computer magazine ads for mail-order suppliers who have toll-free telephone ordering or for discount dealers in the next town will probably inspire you to look for better deals. When one comes along, perhaps at a regional computer show, you may be quick to take advantage of it and buy five times as much as you normally would to save an extra 10 to 15 percent. There's nothing wrong with following that pattern, as long as you exercise some caution when you're buying accessories at the computer store.

Blank Disks

No matter how simply your PC system is configured, you will need some blank disks on hand to make copies of the DOS and applications programs. Blank disks come in many styles, most of which are designed for computers other than the IBM PC or compatibles. This fact can cause no small amount of confusion for an inexperienced disk buyer. And the terminology can often be difficult to comprehend.

Blank disks for the 5¼-inch disk drives of the IBM PC have four primary specifications that differentiate them from others of the same diameter: the number of sides that can be used, the density, the way the disk is sectored, and the number of tracks per inch to be written onto it.

You cannot tell the difference between single- and double-sided disks by looking at them. Some, but not all, manufacturers identify disks as single- or double-sided on the label. But there is a difference, and it lies in the quality of the magnetic media—the actual disk—inside the disk jacket. All disks are tested by the manufacturer to verify that the disk surface contains no flaws; single-sided disks are tested on only one side, while double-sided disks are tested on both sides. Although you can use single-sided disks in double-sided drives, you take the risk that the second, untested side may contain some flaws. Although the DOS will detect and seal off any such flaws on the disk surface, you'll avoid this problem if you buy disks rated with the same number of sides as your disk drives.

Unfortunately, the number of tested sides on the disks inside a box is not always obvious on the outside of the box. A kind of shorthand is often used to describe the contents. One such shorthand notation might read "SS/SD," while another might read "DS/DD." To the untrained eye, there is little distinction between the two notations. The first two letters of this type of notation (to the left of the slash) indicate the number of sides for which the disks are rated—either single-sided (SS) or double-sided (DS). Assuming that you equip your PC with double-sided disk drives, you should use double-sided disks. In the cryptic notation of blank disk boxes, the first two letters should read "DS."

The second disk specification, density, is revealed by the letters to the right of the slash in blank disk notation. You can choose from three types: "SD" (single-density), "DD" (double-density), or "QD" (quad-density). Of the three, only double-density works on the PC. Single-density disks are used in low-capacity (around 150K) disk drives such as those of some home computers. Quad-density disk drives are relatively scarce, as are the blank disks for them.

Putting higher density disks into the PC's disk drives won't give you any more storage space per disk. The amount of information a disk can store is determined by the disk operating system software (DOS). When purchasing disks, specify double-sided, double-density—those labeled "DS/DD."

Another disk specificaton is disk sectors. Each narrow, circular band (track) on the disk is subdivided into sectors—small segments of the track that hold a uniform amount of data (512 bytes for the PC). Some disk drives require disks on which the sectors have been mapped out on the blank disk during manufacturing. A disk with these permanent sector locations is said to be *hard-sectored*. The IBM PC and compatibles don't use this kind of disk, however; they require disks that are *soft-sectored*. The DOS software maps out the sectors on the disk in a procedure known as *formatting*.

The final specification is the disk's tracks per inch. Depending on manufacturing design, double-density disks can be formatted in capacities of either 48 or 96 tracks per inch (tpi). Not many computers use 96 tpi disk drives, but those that do, including the Tandy TRS-80 2000, have twice the storage capacity on a double-sided, double-density disk as the IBM PC and most other compatibles. Until the PC drives are upgraded (if ever), your blank disks should have 48 tracks per inch.

Disk Brands and Prices

Retail prices of blank disks vary so widely that one of the first questions careful shoppers ask is whether the extra money for the more expensive brands buys higher quality disks.

Because the disk surface—the iron oxide coating—looks the same on all disks, differences among brands are not visible. One physical difference, however, is an important one. Some inexpensive disks don't have reinforcing hub rings, which help lengthen the life of a disk, especially if it is used frequently. Hub rings provide a thicker surface for the disk drive spindle to grip as you close the disk drive door (or turn the latch on some drives). The spindle exerts pressure on the disk to keep it from slipping out of its grip when the drive's read/write head comes in contact with the disk. The hub ring prevents the disk from damage at the center where the drive's hub spins it.

Some brands have special liners inside the cardboard jacket to perform minimal dusting. Others are supplied in sturdy boxes. But beyond these more obvious differences, you have little else to go by in selecting a brand.

On some premium brands, you pay a small built-in cost for the manufacturer's warranty. But receiving a free disk to replace one that failed after you've put your annual budget forecast on it is hardly adequate compensation. And since you have the opportunity to back up all floppy disks, disk manufacturers will not accept liability for data lost due to disk failure.

Your computer dealer may assist you in choosing a brand of disks, although you can be sure that only the brands he or she carries will be pushed. If you have friends who are PC users, ask them which brands they use and which ones they've had trouble with in the past.

The best guide, however, will ultimately be your own experience. If you find a budget brand that works consistently—especially after heavy use—stick with it. Focus your bargain-hunting attention on the mail-order houses and discount outlets carrying that brand.

Most disks are sold in boxes of ten. Prices are quoted by the box (about $22 to $60) and by the disk (about $3 to $6). Most dealers have quantity price breaks for five or ten boxes of disks (there are usually ten boxes to a case). Try to buy as large a quantity as possible. Five boxes of disks should last a moderately active PC user one to two years. Someone who uses a PC every day in a professional environment could easily need ten boxes a year. Store unopened boxes in a cool, dry place, and don't remove the cellophane from the box until you need a disk. The longer you can keep dust out of the box, the better.

When you buy your computer, you'll have to figure out how many disks to buy right away. One box (ten disks) should get you through the first week or two, depending on how much software you buy and how much work you plan to do on the computer. You'll need to make at least one backup copy of DOS, plus backup copies of each program (those that aren't copy protected). For most of those programs you will also need at least one data disk to store information (word processing documents, spreadsheet figures, and so on). And if you start experimenting with BASIC, you'll need a disk on which to store those programs.

Because your first box of disks won't last too long, start looking for good buys right away. Never let yourself have fewer than two blank disks in stock before buying more. (Some experienced users would correct that figure to one box of blank disks.) Otherwise, you may find yourself in desperate need of a disk some evening, long after the local store has closed.

Storing Disks

As soon as you start using your second box of disks, you will notice a problem that is guaranteed to multiply as you work with your computer: how to store the disks you work with regularly. The first temptation is to overstuff one of the original cardboard disk boxes. This is not a good policy, because you risk bending a disk while trying to jam it into the box. Look at the size of the box used to get the disks to you. Notice how loosely the disks fit inside. Disk manufacturers intentionally package the disks loosely.

There are several disk storage alternatives. Computer supply and software stores offer many styles of binder storage systems (some looseleaf, others permanently bound) for disks. This method offers an adequate interim solution to the storage problem, but will become unwieldy if you have a lot of program or storage disks that you must locate frequently.

A better solution is a hard plastic storage case. And there are enough varieties around to satisfy most users. Some hold ten disks each and interlock, so that you can build them around your computer as your collection grows. Another kind is designed in a flip-top arrangement, frequently with adjustable dividers. You can find these boxes in sizes that hold up to 75 disks. Variations on the flip-top box have locks and carrying handles.

Eventually, you'll have to face the problem of long-term disk storage for the disks you rarely use. Any plastic storage case is a good candidate for archival storage. Label groups of disks and individual disks well, because you are not likely to remember the intricacies of your filing system when the disks have been stored away for a year. You might also consider fire-protective cabinets for storing valuable archive disks, such as original copies of your applications software. The best place for archival storage, however, is in a building other than the one in which your PC is located. If your computer's building burns down or is swept away by a flood, you'll still have your software and irreplaceable data disks intact.

Printer Paper

If you buy a printer, you will need paper. Computer printer paper comes in enough varieties to satisfy just about every possible application you could have in mind, but it helps to know your options early, before you buy large amounts of paper that you don't need.

Most formed-character printers and the better dot matrix printers let you feed single sheets of regular typing paper or stationery just as you would using a typewriter. We've already discussed the possibility of adding single-sheet feeders to your printer to help automate this process. But single-sheet feeding is the least common way to put paper into a printer.

Much more common is continuous-form paper. It gets its name from the way the sheets are connected by perforations at the top and bottom. At the factory, continuous-form paper is usually folded at the perforations. This process is called *fan folding*, because its fold is reminiscent of that of an oriental fan.

The type of paper you select for your printer depends largely upon the kind of printing work you do. You have many choices: size, preprinted format, weight, paper quality, and even the density of the perforations along the edges.

Computer paper sizes are usually measured by the size of a single sheet with the tractor-feed strips attached. Occasionally, the *trim size*—tractor strips removed—is also provided. Two of the most popular sizes are 9½ by 11 inches (trim size is standard letter size, 8½ by 11 inches) and 14⅞ by 11 inches. The wider size is intended for printers that have extra-wide carriages—those capable of 132-column printing (in a standard, noncompressed font). Wide printers are used most often in accounting, inventory, and other business applications requiring extensive printed reports. Odd paper sizes, such as 11¾ inches wide by 8½ inches high (for printing on 8½-by-11-inch paper sideways) are also available, but mostly from computer supply firms, not as regularly stocked items in computer stores. Most of the printers PC owners use, however, cannot accept wide paper.

Most applications call for blank, white paper. But for some business applications, especially those that produce reams of closely spaced figures, you might consider the green bar type of paper. More common in wider paper sizes than in letter size, green bar paper typically has half-inch light green horizontal bars printed on the paper, alternated with half-inch white areas. You get three single-spaced lines printed on the white background and three lines on the green background. The advantage, especially on the wider paper, is that it lets the reader follow a row of figures more easily across a page. For even more precision, you may find green bar paper that has ⅙-inch bars at ⅙-inch spacing. Because this is the normal line spacing for computer printers (six printed lines per inch), you get alternating lines of white and green background.

All the paper styles discussed so far are available in different weights, from a low of 12 pound to a high of 20 pound. The lighter the paper, the greater the chance that it will jam in the tractor feed, because the device's teeth tend to pull hard on the paper in many printers. A jammed tractor feeder is not the end of the world, but it can be an inconvenience if you're in a hurry to get a job done. For everyday work such as rough drafts, computer program listings, and telecommunications printouts, 15-pound paper usually does the job well. But if you send your work to other people—a final word processing draft to an editor, a printout of a chart for the boss, or financial figures that will get circulated through the office, for example—use 20-pound paper.

A new kind of continuous-form paper is gaining popularity because the perforations barely show. Its very fine perforations on all sides leave the edges smooth. You can get this kind of perforation on bond-quality paper, including some that have a classic laid finish and others that have 25 percent rag content. Some paper distributors, including Uarco, sell this kind of paper in various colors (ivory, tan, light gray, light blue, and so on) and offer to print your letterhead on it. The computer-printed letter (if produced on a formed-character printer) will look as if it had been typed on a typewriter. The producers of continuous-form stationery also offer continuous-form, custom-imprinted envelopes to match.

Paper costs are tied directly to weight and quality. Boxes of computer paper contain from 2500 to 3200 sheets, depending on the weight. You'll find 15-pound paper for under $20 per box for 3200 sheets, while the same quantity of 20-pound finely perforated paper could cost more than $70. You'll more often find perforated, 15-pound paper, since few dealers carry large quantities of finely perforated paper yet. Although a finished product looks much better on higher quality paper, you will have to decide if the extra cost is worthwhile.

Experienced users generally have more than one kind of paper handy, ready to be fed into the printer when the need arises. There's no reason why you can't have finely perforated bond paper for important documents as well as the less-expensive, lighter paper ready for rough drafts and other low-quality printing jobs.

Other Supplies

There's really little else you need to buy when you purchase your computer system. Even if you have a printer, you won't be needing a printer ribbon so soon that you have to buy one with the printer—even the one-time-through multistrike ribbons used by many formed-character printers. But start looking for a discount ribbon supplier who provides a discount for purchase of a dozen or more. Although it's not a good idea to keep too many inked ribbons on hand, because they dry out over time, always have at least two extra ribbons.

Dust covers are appropriate in most environments, but you may want to choose one from a computer magazine rather than buying one from a dealer. Once you feel comfortable with the machine, start looking in the magazines and the stores for accessories. Keep an ample supply of blank disks, paper, and ribbons. Shortages have a way of sneaking up on you at the worst times. Don't get caught with your inventory down.

CHAPTER FIFTEEN

The Computer Room

Few PC buyers plan ahead for the computer's environment before buying a system, but the computer's location is almost as important as hardware and software purchases. Your system will need electrical outlets, desk space, and nearby storage for disks and program manuals. You will also need the right tabletop height, chair adjustment, and lighting.

Ergonomics is the study of work, and recent emphasis has been given to ergonomics as it applies to human-computer interaction. Studies conducted predominantly in European workplaces have determined that keyboard and monitor locations affect the user's posture, viewing comfort, and fatigue. With the proliferation of computer-related equipment in offices, the potential health effects of working with this equipment have prompted some controversial claims and a variety of additional studies. Although the science of computer ergonomics is still in its infancy, you can design certain aspects of the computer setup to encourage comfort, safety, and efficiency.

Keyboard Placement
The detached keyboard of the IBM PC and most compatibles offers positioning flexibility. The fact that you can move it within the limit of the connecting cord enables you to reposition it during a computing session.

Most PC-standard keyboards also have a low-profile design—the keytops are closer to the table than those of the fixed keyboards built into a computer's cabinet. You don't have to raise your arms too high for comfort or arch your wrists unnaturally to reach the keyboard.

Placing a computer on a standard desk is not recommended if you plan to do a lot of keyboard work, particularly word processing. Most desks are 29 inches high, which is comfortable for writing, but a typing surface should be lower. Having the keyboard at 29 inches makes you lift your shoulders and wrists, just as if you had a fixed-keyboard computer. Most typing tables are 26 to 27 inches high. Although a 2- or 3-inch difference may not sound like much, it can be significant when applied to keyboard height.

You have some options in positioning the keyboard at this 26- to 27-inch height, but they involve buying new furniture. One option is adding a typing-height extension (often called a return) to an existing office desk, forming an L-shaped desk arrangement. A simpler solution, especially in an executive office or the home environment, is to buy a computer work station from a computer and office furniture outlet. You can buy a 27-inch-high table, a 29-inch-high table that has an adjustable pedestal for the keyboard, or a desk that has a sliding tray for the keyboard.

Computer furniture tends to be modular in nature. You can start with a table and later add drawer units, corner connectors, and other tables to build a substantial working area as your needs grow. Your best long-term buys will be with modular styles, because they can grow as your computer use increases.

Monitor Placement

You almost always see the IBM PC displayed with the monitor atop the System Unit. Although this arrangement makes the IBM PC look compact on the desk, it may not be the best place for it.

One of the major health problems associated with computer work is eye fatigue caused by both excessive motion of the eyes from a source document to the screen and the eye adjustments involved in looking at dark type on light paper and light type on a dark screen. Ideally, you want as little eye movement as possible. The amount of eye movement you will have depends upon whether your work involves looking from paper to screen and how you orient the source document on the desk.

European-designed computers generally have the monitor low on the desk—on the desktop or on a slim console. By experimenting with such an arrangement, you might find that there is less strain on your eyes when you look down at about a 40- to 45-degree angle—where the monitor would be if it were not sitting on top of the System Unit.

With the monitor resting on the desktop, you should be able to position the face of the screen so that it tilts to your line of sight. You can buy a pedestal that lets you adjust the tilt and rotation of the monitor for this purpose. Oddly enough, some users place their monitors on pedestals on top of their System Units, an arrangement that raises the monitor even higher than when it rests on the System Unit by itself.

IBM PC monitors are separate units that can be turned and tilted as needed. Computers that have built-in screens, however, including the portables, cannot be adjusted as easily. Keep this in mind if you are considering a computer with a built-in monitor.

Glare is another potential problem with monitors that can make work difficult. Glare results when light from either fixtures or windows reflects off the screen. It is what a photographer would call a hot spot—a burst of bright light on an otherwise dark background. Although you may not actually focus on the hot spot, it partially obscures the text or the graphics you're trying to view on the monitor. Your eyes strain to filter out the hot spot and concentrate on the screen's contents.

In many offices light comes from so many different sources and angles that the usual solution, tilting or swiveling the monitor, won't eliminate the problem. Even the etched surface of the IBM Monochrome Display can't entirely eliminate glare.

Some independent suppliers have developed special glare filters, or shields, that fit over the screen area of the Monochrome Display and other monitors (see Figure 15.1). They not only enhance the green phosphor of the display but also reduce glare. If your work area is subject to glare, don't hesitate to add this low-cost accessory. Color monitors, with their traditionally glossy screen finishes, require special planning and care to avoid glare, particularly from bright light coming in through a window. A windowless room that has adjustable incandescent lighting is the most comfortable viewing environment.

Cords and Cables

When it comes to discussing cords and cables for the PC, the self-contained portables that have built-in monitors and printers seem quite attractive. All you have to do is plug in one power cord, and you've installed the entire system. Unfortunately, it's not as easy with most PC-standard computers.

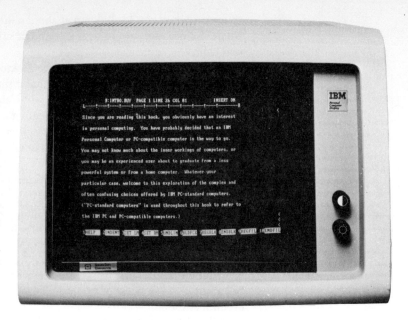

Figure 15.1 *The IBM Mono-chrome Display with a glare shield (left) and the same text on the screen without a glare shield (right).*

In a PC or XT system that includes the IBM Monochrome Display and a printer, you will need two power outlets: one for the System Unit and another for the printer. The System Unit has a special connector built into it that passes 120 volts AC to the Monochrome Display, which plugs directly into the System Unit with a special power cord that cannot be plugged directly into an ordinary 120 VAC power outlet. Color monitors and some other monochrome monitors require an additional outlet for the monitor's cord.

Power cords for the PC and XT System Units, as well as for just about every printer you'll find, are the three-pronged, grounded type. You'll need grounded power outlets for them. Don't attempt to use the equipment with power cord adapters that bypass the ground and plug into standard two-pronged household sockets. Because commercial buildings use grounded outlets almost exclusively, you shouldn't have difficulty finding the proper kind of outlet in an office building. And most residential builders are now installing grounded outlets throughout houses.

An associated problem with power outlets is getting enough to go around. If your system consists of an IBM PC, a printer, a color monitor, and an external modem, you will need four outlets. The power cable for the modem may be a transformer type with the plug built into a small black box. This box-type plug may cover up one or more other outlets.

To provide more outlets, you can use what is called a power strip, which usually has a heavy-duty extension cord to connect it to a grounded outlet. Some models in the $20 to $30 range provide six grounded outlets, often with a switch to turn them on or off.

Power-Line Suppressors and Filters

A potential hazard for computer users are fluctuations in the power lines coming into homes or offices. Underpowering your computer a bit won't hurt it (unless the power is so low that you lose information), but power spikes or surges will. A spike is a sudden bolt of power for a very short period of time, such as 5000 volts for less than a millionth of a second. A spike can occur when the power company switches a new generator on line or restores power after an outage. Or a strong lightning bolt near a utility pole (it doesn't even have to hit it) can send a spike of electromagnetic radiation measuring thousands of volts down your power lines (they act like a big receiving antenna) and damage some sensitive components—even if the computer is turned off. A surge, the longer lasting relative of a power spike, can also destroy the data in RAM or damage the computer if the surge is strong enough.

Another source of trouble in power lines is noise. Other appliances—even other computer components such as printers—sharing the same internal power line can send interfering signals over that line. If they are strong enough, these signals can interfere with the computer's operation.

A particular offender is the cordless telephone. A cordless phone uses the power line as an antenna to send voice and ringing signals to the hand-held unit. A ringing cordless phone plugged into the same power strip as an IBM PC can send extraneous signals that could appear on the screen as keystrokes. The resulting keystrokes may even cause the computer to freeze up.

Although you can prevent the problems caused by power-line interference, you have to be aware of exactly what kind of problems you have. If you are located in a thunderstorm belt, you'll be safer during the storm season if you have some kind of surge protection in your power line. You may already know if your location is subject to voltage spikes. If you've ever had a television or other electronic device get zapped for no apparent reason, your power lines may be subject to spikes from the power company, and you should invest in a surge protector early on.

If your computer shares its power circuit with noisy appliances, such as hair dryers and cordless phones, a line filter is a good investment. There is very little you can do to detect line noise except to wait for it to do some damage to your data. If the appliance interference problem attacks your computer, you can either try to track down the offending appliance and disconnect it, or invest in a power-line noise filter.

When shopping for power-line protection, be aware that surges and noises are two different problems. Only a few of the protection devices available offer both surge and noise protection in one package.

When considering surge protectors, look for models that start functioning at a *clamping voltage* (the point at which the protection equipment intercepts the power in case of overvoltage) just above the computer's nominal 120 VAC. A surge protector whose clamping voltage is more than 130 volts, for example, does not provide adequate protection. If you make sure that the device works up to at least 10,000 volts, your machine should be able to withstand just about everything but a direct bolt from Zeus.

If you don't have a surge suppressor and you experience a power outage, turn off the computer and, preferably, unplug it from the wall socket. When power is restored, there may be a voltage spike, and unplugging your system will protect it from this source of damage.

Computer Placement

As noted previously, it may be easier on your eyes if you place the monitor on the desktop instead of the System Unit. Unfortunately, the length of the IBM Monochrome Display's cable doesn't offer much flexibility in that regard. Neither of the monitor's two cables is long enough to let you position the monitor very far from the System Unit. You can, however, buy extension cables from independent suppliers so that you can separate the System Unit and the monitor.

You can save space by putting the System Unit under the desk, but remember that you will need access to the disk drives. This is especially true with the standard PC, because you won't be able to run a program without putting in at least one disk. With the XT, if your programs and stored data are all kept on the fixed disk, you can get away with placing the System Unit in a less convenient location. But even with an XT, you should not block off the System Unit, because you should be frequently backing up the hard disk on floppies (unless you have another external backup device).

Mounting the System Unit vertically on the side of the desk is both attractive and space saving. Stands are available that enable you to place the System Unit securely on its side (with the power switch facing up), and the disk drives function well in a vertical position. Just be sure to have the disk drives at the top. They'll be easy to reach and further away from dust and dirt at floor level, and you'll have easy access to the computer's power switch.

Be prepared for a slight shock when you bring the PC into your office. For some reason, the System Unit seems larger in the office than it looks in the store. Before you buy a computer, know exactly where you're going to put the System Unit and the keyboard. You must add to those dimensions a bit, too, because you'll need several inches behind the System Unit (if you intend to park it in front of a wall) for the cables and the connectors that will be attached to it. An IBM PC System Unit and keyboard just barely fit on a 24-inch-deep desktop—and only then if the desk is pulled two to three inches away from the wall to accommodate cables. That puts the keyboard right up against the front of the desk, giving you no extra work room in front of the computer. It's best to have the computer on a table separate from your regular desk.

Printer Placement

PC printers generally come in two sizes: moderately big, like the IBM Graphics Printer, and outrageously big, like the NEC and Diablo formed-character printers. All printers require a cable that connects them to the PC. Because printer cables are generally 6- to 12-feet long, you will have flexibility in setting up the printer.

With the exception of thermal, ink jet, and laser printers, which few people presently use with a PC, printers are loud. Although you will probably want to have the printer as far away from your work area as possible, you will have to station it close enough to be able to check it frequently. Whether you keep the printer nearby or halfway across the room will depend upon your personal taste and the amount of hand feeding of paper you will be doing. Some suppliers offer printer covers that effectively muffle the printer's noise. These units are expensive (usually $500 or more), cumbersome, and may not be available to fit every brand of printer.

Formed-character printers are not only loud, but send a tremor through the table on which they are placed. The precise start-and-stop motion of the printhead and the impact of the hammer on each printing element cause considerable vibration that can become annoying if you are trying to do something besides printing on the same table. Formed-character printers operate best on a separate table.

Most formed-character printers (and some dot matrix printers) allow paper to be fed from beneath the printer. If you have a printer table that has a slit in the middle, you can store a box of printer paper under the table and feed it straight up through the table top to the printer. Such printer tables usually have accessory baskets that hook onto the rear of the table to catch the printouts.

Unfortunately, no one has effectively solved the paper-catching problem for a printer located on a table against the wall. For long printouts, you'll probably have to drape the paper over the front of the printer and have it land on the floor in front of the printer table.

Ventilation

Computer components need ventilation. You have probably noticed vertical slits on the front panel. Those holes are critical to the System Unit's overall cooling system. The internal fan, even though it is located at the opposite corner, draws air into the System Unit through the holes. Don't block them. There are more slits in the back of the unit for the exhaust of the fan. Fortunately, the cables at the rear of the System Unit prevent you from shoving the console too close to a wall. You need those extra few inches for ventilation.

Monitors do not contain cooling fans, but rely on a natural convection cooling system to control temperature. As the components inside a monitor heat up, the hot air surrounding them rises through the holes at the top of the cabinet. To replace that air, cool air automatically flows in through the holes in the bottom of the cabinet. Don't block either the bottom or the top holes.

Printers can also heat up. As long as you keep plenty of free space around them, however, they should stay cool, even during long printing sessions.

Shelf Space

In addition to reserving space for your computer and printer, be sure to set aside desk or shelf space close by for the software manuals that you'll accumulate. Many software manuals imitate the style made popular by IBM: three-ringed binders measuring approximately 9 by 8 inches. Spine width varies from manual to manual. IBM manuals are supplied in slipcases, which make stacking them easy. When you buy an IBM PC or XT, you get three manuals: the *Guide to Operations,* a DOS reference manual, and a BASIC reference manual. Add to this at least one fat manual per applications program.

Not every software supplier follows the binder/slipcase format, however. Although sizes vary, be prepared, within an arm's reach of your work station, for at least two linear feet of binders as tall as standard three-ring binders. This should give you enough room for later growth, especially if you vertically stack the binders that come with slipcases.

Appendix: Products and Manufacturers

Following are products mentioned in this book. The memory requirements for software assume DOS 2.00. Note that these programs do not necessarily run on all PC-standard computers. Contact the manufacturer for further information.

Software

1-2-3
Lotus Development Corporation
161 First St.
Cambridge, MA 02142
617/492-7171
Requirements: 192K, two disk drives, color graphics board or dot matrix printer for graphics component

dBASE II
Ashton-Tate
10150 W. Jefferson Blvd.
Culver City, CA 90230
213/204-5570
Requirements: 128K, one disk drive

EasyWriter II System
Information Unlimited Software
2401 Marinship Way
Sausalito, CA 94965
415/331-6700
Requirements: 128K, two disk drives

Flight Simulator
Microsoft Corporation
10700 Northup Way
Bellevue, WA 98004
206/828-8080
Requirements: 64K, one disk drive, IBM Color/Graphics Adapter, composite monitor for color

Jack2
Business Solutions, Inc.
60 E. Main St.
Kings Park, NY 11754
516/269-1120
Requirements: 128K, two disk drives, has own operating system

MBA
Context Management Systems
23868 Hawthorne Blvd.
Torrance, CA 90505
213/378-8277
Requirements: 256K, two disk drives, IBM Color/Graphics Adapter

Microsoft Windows
Microsoft Corporation
10700 Northup Way
Bellevue, WA 98004
206/828-8080
Requirements: 192K, two disk drives, pointing device

MultiMate
MultiMate International
52 Oakland Ave. N
East Hartford, CT 06108
203/522-2116
Requirements: 256K, two disk drives

Multiplan
Microsoft Corporation
10700 Northup Way
Bellevue, WA 98004
206/828-8080
Requirements: 128K, one disk drive

Ovation Software
Ovation Technologies
320 Norwood Park S
Norwood, MA 02062
617/769-9300
Requirements: 512K, hard disk, IBM Color/Graphics Adapter

Pac-Man
Atarisoft
P.O. Box 61657
1312 Crossman Ave.
Sunnyvale, CA 94088
800/538-8543, 800/672-1404 in California
Requirements: 128K, color graphics board

PC-Talk III
The Headlands Press, Inc.
P.O. Box 862
Tiburon, CA 94920
415/435-9775
Requirements: 64K (128K for compiled version), one disk drive

PC Tutor
Comprehensive Software
2810 Artesia Blvd.
Redondo Beach, CA 90278
213/318-2561, 213/214-1461
Requirements: 64K, one disk drive

pfs:file, pfs:report
Software Publishing Corporation
1901 Landings Dr.
Mountain View, CA 94043
415/962-8910
Requirements: 128K, one disk drive

SuperCalc
Sorcim Corporation
2310 Lundy Ave.
San Jose, CA 95131
408/942-1727
Requirements: 64K, one disk drive

SuperCalc3
Sorcim Corporation
2310 Lundy Ave.
San Jose, CA 95131
408/942-1727
Requirements: 96K, one disk drive

Symphony
Lotus Development Corporation
161 First St.
Cambridge, MA 02142
800/343-5414, 617/492-7870 in
Massachusetts
Requirements: 320K, one disk drive

VisiCalc
VisiCorp
2895 Zanker Rd.
San Jose, CA 95134
408/946-9000, 408/942-6000 (customer
support)
Requirements: 64K, one disk drive

VisiCalc IV
VisiCorp
2895 Zanker Rd.
San Jose, CA 95134
408/946-9000, 408/942-6000 (customer
support)
Requirements: 128K (192K to use sorting
function), one disk drive

Visi On
VisiCorp
2895 Zanker Rd.
San Jose, CA 95134
408/946-9000, 408/942-6000 (customer
support)
Requirements: 512K, one floppy disk
drive, one hard disk, graphics board and
graphics monitor to run windows

Volkswriter
Lifetree Software, Inc.
411 Pacific St. #315
Monterey, CA 93940
408/373-4718
Requirements: 64K, one disk drive

WordStar
MicroPro International Corporation
33 San Pablo Ave.
San Rafael, CA 94903
415/499-1200
Requirements: 64K, one disk drive

Computers

Apricot
ACT Ltd.
3375 Scott Blvd. #336
Santa Clara, CA 95051
408/727-8639

Chameleon, Chameleon Plus
Seequa Computer Corporation
8305 Telegraph Rd.
Odenton, MD 21113
800/638-6066, 301/672-3600

Columbia MPC, Columbia VP
Columbia Data Products
9150 Rumsey Rd.
Columbia, MD 21045
301/992-3400

Commuter
Visual Computer, Inc.
135 Maple St.
Marlboro, MA 01752
617/480-0000

Compaq, Compaq-Plus
Compaq Computer Corporation
12330 Perry Rd.
Houston, TX 77070
713/890-7390

Corona PC, Portable PC
Corona Data Systems
31324 Via Colinas #110
Westlake Village, CA 91361
213/707-0672

Eagle PC Plus series
Eagle Computer, Inc.
983 University Ave.
Los Gatos, CA 95030
408/395-5005

Gavilan
Gavilan Computer Corporation
240 Hacienda Ave.
Campbell, CA 95008
408/379-8000

HP-150
Hewlett-Packard
16399 W. Bernardo Dr.
San Diego, CA 92127
800/367-4722 (FOR-HPCC)

Hyperion
Bytec-Comterm, Inc.
8 Colonnade Rd.
Ottawa, Ontario
K2E7M6 Canada
613/226-7255

IBM PC, XT, Portable PC, PCjr
IBM
System Products Division
P.O. Box 1328
Boca Raton, FL 33432
800/447-4700, 332-4400 in Illinois,
800/447-0890 in Alaska and Hawaii

Leading Edge PC
Leading Edge Products, Inc.
225 Turnpike St.
Canton, MA 03032
617/828-8150

PC Traveler
Strategic Technologies, Inc.
7001 Peachtree Industrial Blvd., Bldg. 3
Norcross, GA 30071
404/441-8070

Pronto
Pronto Computers, Inc.
3730 Skypark Dr.
Torrance, CA 90505
213/539-6400

Sperry PC
Sperry Corporation
P.O. Box 500
Blue Bell, PA 19424
215/542-4459

Sr. Partner
Panasonic
One Panasonic Way
Secaucus, NJ 07094
201/348-7182

Tandy TRS-80 2000
Radio Shack Computer Customer Service
400 Atrium, One Tandy Center
Fort Worth, TX 76102
817/390-3011

TI Professional Computer
Texas Instruments Incorporated
P.O. Box 402430
Dallas, TX 75240
800/527-3500

XTRA
ITT Courier Terminal Systems, Inc.
1515 S. 14th St.
Tempe, AZ 85281
602/894-7797

Miscellaneous Hardware

Corvus hard disk
Corvus Systems, Inc.
2100 Corvus Dr.
San Jose, CA 95124
408/559-7000

Epson printers
Epson America, Inc.
3415 Kashiwa St.
Torrance, CA 90505
800/421-5426, 213/539-9140 in California

Hercules Graphics Card
Hercules Computer Technology
2550 Ninth St. #210
Berkeley, CA 94710
415/540-6000

NEC 3550 printer
NEC Information Systems, Inc.
1414 Massachusetts Ave.
Boxborough, MA 01719
800/343-4418

Smartmodem
Hayes Microcomputer Products, Inc.
5923 Peachtree Industrial Blvd.
Norcross, GA 30092
404/441-1617

TI 855 microprinter
Texas Instruments Incorporated
P.O. Box 402430
Dallas, TX 75240
800/527-3500

Danny Goodman is a Contributing Editor to *PC World, Creative Computing,* and *Radio-Electronics* magazines. He is the author of *The Simon & Schuster Guide to the Radio Shack Model 100, The Simon & Schuster Guide to the IBM PCjr,* and *The Simon & Schuster Guide to the Apple Macintosh (Simon & Schuster, 1984), Word Processing on the IBM Personal Computer* (Howard W. Sams, 1983), and *A Parents' Guide to Personal Computers and Software* (Touchstone/Simon & Schuster, 1983). Danny Goodman appears frequently as personal computer and electronics commentator on the Public Broadcasting Service television series, "The New Tech Times." His articles on computers and electronics appear in *Playboy, Better Homes & Gardens, Chicago, Consumers Digest,* and other publications.

The following people contributed to this book:

Editor: Jeremy Joan Hewes; *Consulting Editors, PC World:* David Bunnell, Andrew Fluegelman; *Consulting Editor, Simon & Schuster:* Robert C. Eckhardt; *PC World Books Editorial staff:* Betsy Dilernia, Lindy Wankoff, Evelyn Spire, Joanne Clapp; *Production Director:* Jacqueline Poitier; *Designer:* Marjorie Spiegelman; *Art Director:* Bruce Charonnat; *Production and Art staff:* Ellyn Hament, Jim Felici, Rebecca Oliver, Art Wilcox, Dennis McLeod, Monica Thorsnes, Darcy Blake, Donna Sharee, Molly Windsor-McLeod; *Photographer:* Jeffery Newbury; *Cover Photographer:* Fred Stimson; *Typesetter:* Design & Type, San Francisco.

The photograph on page 37 is reproduced by courtesy of Tecmar, Inc.

Each of the following products is a trademark or a registered trademark of the company listed in parentheses after the product name.

Software
1-2-3, Symphony (Lotus Development Corporation), *dBASE II* (Ashton-Tate), *EasyWriter II System* (Information Unlimited Software), *Flight Simulator, Microsoft Windows* (Microsoft Corporation), *Jack2* (Business Solutions, Inc.), *MBA* (Context Management Systems), *Microsoft Windows* (Microsoft Corporation), *Multiplan* (Microsoft Corporation), *MultiMate* (MultiMate International), *Ovation Software* (Ovation Technologies), *Pac-Man* (Atarisoft), *PC-Talk III* (The Headlands Press, Inc.), *PC Tutor* (Comprehensive Software), *pfs:file, pfs:report* (Software Publishing Corporation), *SuperCalc, SuperCalc3* (Sorcim Corporation), *VisiCalc, VisiCalc IV, Visi On* (VisiCorp), *Volkswriter* (Lifetree Software, Inc.), *WordStar* (MicroPro International Corporation).

Hardware
Apricot (ACT Ltd.), Chameleon, Chameleon Plus, (Seequa Computer Corporation), Columbia MPC, Columbia VP, (Columbia Data Products), Commuter (Visual Computer, Inc.), Compaq, Compaq-Plus, (Compaq Computer Corporation), Corona PC, Portable PC, (Corona Data Systems), Corvus hard disk (Corvus Systems, Inc.), Eagle PC Plus, (Eagle Computer, Inc.), Epson (Epson America, Inc.), Gavilan (Gavilan Computer Corporation), Hercules Graphics Card (Hercules Computer Technology), HP-150 (Hewlett-Packard), Hyperion (Bytec-Comterm, Inc.), Leading Edge PC (Leading Edge Products, Inc.), NEC 3550 (NEC Information Systems, Inc.), PC Traveler (Strategic Technologies, Inc.), Pronto (Pronto Computers,

Index

Page numbers in italic indicate definitions.

Other
PC World Books

Getting Started with the IBM PC and XT

by David Arnold and the Editors of PC World

In *Getting Started with the IBM PC and XT,* David Arnold and the Editors of *PC World* have teamed up to give PC users a clearly written, authoritative guide to using the PC and its more powerful cousin, the XT. If you are new to the computer, you will value the tutorial approach to becoming familiar with the keyboard, the disks, and the disk operating system (DOS 1.10 and 2.00) and to learning how to set up and handle electronic files. You will appreciate the careful explanations of how to evaluate your software needs and the practical introduction to BASIC, which includes essential commands for file management as well as programming. If you are already working with the PC or the XT and want to explore further, you can count on *Getting Started* for detailed explanations and examples of advanced aspects of DOS 2.00 and special XT requirements, such as hard disk formatting. The book also includes a section on the maintenance and care of electronic equipment. Whether you're just beginning to use a PC or need a handy reference manual, this book will help you master the many facets of your computer and keep it running smoothly.

Getting Started with the IBM PCjr

by David Myers and the Editors of PC World

In the same way that the IBM PC has become the dominant force in person computers, the IBM Home Computer—the PCjr—is emerging as an equally exciting and impressive force among family oriented machines. To introduce you to the PCjr and to computing in general, David Myers and the Editors of PC World have applied their expertise to describing this fascinating machine, providing you and your family with the perfect guide to making the most of the PCjr. *Getting Started with the IBM PCjr* includes detailed and easy-to-understand instructions for using the cordless keyboard, color monitors and television sets for graphics displays, the disk operating system, cartridge and disk-based software, and the most important peripherals that expand the PCjr's capabilities, such as printers, light pens, modems, and joysticks. Special features of the PCjr are highlighted by hands-on tutorials covering graphics and music, and BASIC and Logo. The book also explains how to access information services such as The Source and CompuServe. *Getting Started with the IBM PCjr* will enable you to make home computing one of life's simple pleasures.

Available October 1984*

Desktop Applications for the IBM PC and XT

by Patrick Plemmons and the Editors of PC World

Most people buy a personal computer for one activity, such as word processing, financial calculations, or information management. In doing so, they fail to use the computer's innate capacity to perform other types of tasks equally efficiently and effectively. *Desktop Applications for the IBM PC and XT* demonstrates the amazing breadth and power of the PC and helps you take advantage of the computer's potential as both a personal and a professional tool. The book explains in clear and comprehensive terms the principal categories of professional computer applications: spreadsheets, word processing, data base management, accounting and financial programs, graphics, and integrated software, which is able to perform several applications and transfer information quickly and easily between applications. The authors show you how to make the best use of the computer to execute these tasks. You will learn about the major software packages in each applications category and how to match tasks with the appropriate software. *Desktop Applications for the IBM PC and XT* is certain to expand your knowledge of computing and the uses for your PC or XT.

Available October 1984*

Communications for the IBM PC and XT

by Lisa B. Stahr and the Editors of PC World

One of the truly exciting features of personal computers is their ability to exchange information with each other—and with distant mainframe computers—over the telephone lines. *Communications for the IBM PC and XT* provides a window to resources that extend beyond your PC. Clear, comprehensive and thought-provoking, the book explains how to select the most appropriate modem and communications software for your PC and offers a nontechnical look at how computers communicate with one another. The authors explain how to use the different types of communications to best suit your professional and personal needs, including conducting research on commercial data bases; acquiring software—sometimes for free—by downloading it over the phone lines; sending and receiving messages on an electronic bulletin board; and linking several PCs and XTs into a local area network so that you and your group can access each other's information and perform your work more efficiently than ever. No matter what your specific needs, *Communications for the IBM PC and XT* will help you make the most of your computer's ability to join forces with other computers.

Available November 1984*

Hardware for the IBM PC and XT

by Frederic E. Davis and the Editors of PC World

Hardware for the IBM PC and XT is an invaluable guide and reference that will help you make sense of the continually expanding and sometimes perplexing array of add-on equipment available for the PC, XT, and PC-compatible computers. If you're a newcomer to the PC, the general introductions to peripherals— from such familiar items as keyboards, game controllers, and monitors to more exotic things such as voice recognition devices, bubble memory, and graphics plotters—will provide the basis for understanding each type of hardware. If you already know how you want to expand your system, you can consult the comprehensive listings of the major brand-name products to narrow your choices. Each product listing contains a complete description of the peripheral and its capabilities, as well as a discussion of the important criteria for evaluating features. Also included are sections on troubleshooting problems that might occur with peripherals and designing efficient computer work areas. *Hardware for the IBM PC and XT* opens up new worlds of personal computing by helping you expand your system sensibly, efficiently, and precisely to your needs.

Available January 1985*

Learning and Having Fun with the IBM PC and PCjr

by Fred D'Ignazio and the Editors of PC World

You may think the IBM PC is all work and no play—not true! *Learning and Having Fun with the IBM PC and PCjr* is a delightful, informative look at the vast array of educational and recreational software available for the IBM PC and PCjr. Fred D'Ignazio and the Editors of PC World look at the main areas of educational and recreational computing—from math and spelling programs to mind-boggling adventures and sophisticated tutorials. They provide the criteria for determining what constitutes a good game or learning program and evaluate the best and most important software available today. The book contains hands-on examples of games and educational programs that will enable you to take advantage of the many features of the PC and PCjr and design your own games. Take a break from your spreadsheets and data bases, don your aviator glasses, or strap on Excalibur—and start *Learning and Having Fun with the IBM PC and PCjr.*

Available February 1985*

The Fully Powered PC

by Burton L. Alperson, Andrew Fluegelman, Lawrence J. Magid, and the Editors of PC World

Now that you own a PC and have been working with it for some time, are you starting to wish it had just a few more special features to help you do your job better? Perhaps a way to execute a command in one keystroke that now take six? Or a way to make a section of internal memory act like a disk—but fifty times faster? Are you running out of expansion slots, even though you can think of a dozen more boards you'd like to add? Relax—and read *The Fully Powered PC*, the first and only guide devoted exclusively to ways of customizing the highly versatile PC with modestly priced software and hardware additions, including keyboard reconfiguration programs, spoolers, custom-designed menus, batch filers, and multi-function expansion boards (to squeeze even more capabilities into one expansion slot). With up-to-the-minute guidance from the experts, you'll be able to create a computer system exactly as you want it. When you're ready to take full advantage of your computing capabilities, shift into high gear with *The Fully Powered PC.*

Available March 1985*

Logo for the IBM PC and PCjr

by David Myers and the Editors of PC World

As the personal computer revolution spreads, more and more computer owners have become aware of Logo, which is rapidly emerging as the language of choice for teaching children the fundamentals of computers, programming, and logical thinking. But did you know that Logo is not just for children, and that it's not just a language that makes it easy to create graphics on your computer? *Logo for the IBM PC and PCjr* leads adults and children alike into the world of Logo programming. The book shows you how this elegant, easy-to-learn language can be used to both understand computers and create practical programs that are not available commercially. Using a hands-on, tutorial approach, David Myers and the Editors of PC World take you beyond most other books on Logo, explaining clearly and completely the many fascinating features of this language, including creating turtle graphics, animating sprites, learning how to define your own Logo commands, and even programming your PC or PCjr to converse with you in plain English. And, of course, *Logo for the IBM PC and PCjr* is filled with many sample Logo programs that are both practical and fun.

Available Spring 1985*

Hands On: Useful Tips and Routines for the IBM PC and XT

by the Editors of PC World

For everyone who enjoys the vast number of practical tips and useful articles that have appeared in PC World since its first issue, the Editors of PC World have collected the best of the "Hands On" and "Star-Dot-Star" sections of the magazine. This book covers both hardware and software, and it is clearly organized so that you can quickly find information on virtually anything you need to know about your PC: instructions for installing boards and disk drives, troubleshooting hardware problems, patching programs to utilize the special features of various printers, and increasing programming efficiency. Additional chapters of the book detail specific program applications, such as creating a checkbook ledger with Lotus *1-2-3,* printing envelopes, labels, and other odd-sized documents with *WordStar,* keeping tax records on *dBASE II,* and tracking investments with *SuperCalc. Hands On* is the definitive collection of "how-to's" for your PC from the experts in the field, the Editors of PC World.

Available Spring 1985*

*Publication date subject to change.

☐ **Getting Started with the IBM PC and XT**
by David Arnold and the Editors of PC World
49277-2 $14.95

☐ **How to Buy an IBM PC, XT, or PC-Compatible Computer**
by Danny Goodman and the Editors of PC World
49282-9 $14.95

☐ **Getting Started with the the IBM PCjr**
by David Myers and the Editors of PC World
49253-5 $14.95   Available October 1984

☐ **Desktop Applications for the IBM PC and XT**
by Patrick Plemmons and the Editors of PC World
49279-9 $16.95   Available October 1984

Prices subject to change without notice.
(If not completely satisfied, you may return the books
for full refund within ten days.)

Simon & Schuster, Inc.
Simon & Schuster Building, 1230 Avenue of the Americas
New York, N.Y. 10020, Mail Order Dept. CP9

Please send me copies of the books checked above.

☐ Please charge to my credit card. _____ MasterCard _____ Visa

My credit card number is _____ and expires _____

Signature _____

☐ Save! I enclose a check for the full amount; publisher pays postage and handling.

Name (please print) _____

Address _____

City _____ State _____ Zip Code _____

Also available at your local bookstore.